Defending Capitalism

By Robert Villegas

Defending Capitalism
By Robert Villegas

ISBN: 9798302772060
Imprint: Independently published

Published in the United States of America by Robert Villegas

Email: robertv1989@outlook.com
Social Media Addresses

Blog: https://v4vendata.blogspot.com
CloutHub @RobertVillegas
MeWe www.mewe.com/i/robertvillegas
Minds @Robertv1989
Gab @V4Vendata
GETTR @V4Vendata
WIMKIN Robert Villegas
X: RobertVillegasJ

Dedicated to

Gia Rae

Table of Contents

Defending Capitalism

By Robert Villegas

The goal of this booklet is to introduce young people to the economic system known as capitalism. It is my contention that capitalism is the best economic system in the world. The benefits of capitalism have been left out of the discussion in our universities, and I consider this a travesty. In fact, most college professors today know that if young people were to become aware of the benefits of capitalism, they would reject fascism, communism and socialism, each of which are coercive in nature. Scholars, college professors, and politicians today (properly called pragmatists) have engaged in a virtual desecration of capitalism by means of misrepresenting it's better aspects and endeavoring to poison young minds against the greatest wealth-building system in the history of the world. My point here is that capitalism should be the system of the future, and I will show why capitalism is the only solution for today's economic ills.

Capitalism is an economic system designed to create wealth in society. The study of economics deals with the effective use of capital and how citizens can benefit from the cumulative effects of millions of people simultaneously engaged in trade. The study of capitalism by economists analyzes how to grow wealth and establish human flourishing in society. In my book, *Capitalism Doesn't Fail*[1], I outlined the features of an effective capitalist system:

- Mass Production
- Division of Labor
- Law of Supply and Demand
- Capital Accumulation
- The Free Flow of Capital
- Corporate Structure
- Monetary Policy
- The Principle of Trade

In this book, I showed that economics is the general study of how wealth is produced, utilized, and multiplied in society. Likewise, in his book entitled *Human Action*[2], Ludwig von Mises taught us how to firmly establish the principles of human action in society on the foundation of capitalism. Additionally, In her book, *Capitalism: the Unknown Ideal*[3], Ayn Rand shows that capitalism is based upon individualism as opposed to the various collectivist, altruist, and tribalist views (all of which are parasitic). Individualism is the focus on the individual and his means of survival which is reason. Let us proceed.

[1] https://amzn.to/3EkntJ5
[2] https://amzn.to/40VXv7A
[3] https://amzn.to/42Humyt

The economic system known as capitalism derives from a focus on the individual (as opposed to the collective). The study of capitalism helps us understand not only how the individual thrives in society but also how to structure politics in society. In fact, we understand capitalism by comparing individualism to collectivism and how each of these concepts functions in society.

From individualism comes knowledge that yields informed action and the accomplishment of self-interest. This is why individualism and capitalism are the necessary perspectives for identifying the "proper" principles of thought and action. This yields an understanding of a proper capitalist system (not corrupted by coercion of any kind) and collectivism that is characterized by altruism, tribalism, and their harmful derivative coercions.

Force is the principle that seeks to turn a truly free capitalist system into fascism[4]. Fascism removes freedom from society and turns men against each other through the principles of realpolitik (pragmatism[5]) and "the end justifies the means".

---

[4] Fascism is the imposition of coercive government (socialism and socialist regulations) over an economic system based upon market principles.

[5] Pragmatism is an approach to philosophy that assesses the truth of meaning of theories or beliefs in terms of the success of their practical application. – Oxford Languages

Capitalism, on the other hand, is based upon self-interest and is the only solution to the problems caused by collectivism/fascism/socialism. Self-interest holds that the individual can work for his or her own benefit without government interference.

Indeed, self-interest should be considered an individual right. It should not be the evil scourge that most people today consider it to be. It is a highly moral concept that liberates the individual to act rationally, to do well, and to pursue survival without owing the fruits of his labor to anyone.

A self-interested individual is characterized by an independent mind. He or she questions everything and leaves no leaf unturned in the pursuit of knowledge. Through independence, an individual studies philosophy and history to gain the knowledge needed to organize society, structure the principles of trade, create science, build prosperity, and establish the creation of wealth. Man does these things because he wants to build a better life for himself and those he loves.

Reason[6] enables the individual to learn the principles of trade. It recognizes that men must trade values if they are to succeed, that those values must provide

---

[6] Reason is the power of the mind to think, understand, and form judgments by a process of logic. — Oxford Languages

benefits and be worth the amount of money spent to acquire them. Through reason, the sky is the limit to what a man can do. The four principles of success become: 1. Envision value; 2. Produce value; 3. Educate the customer; and 4. Deliver the value and collect the reward. Once men know how to live, how to trade, how to succeed, they must make sure society is sufficiently free and safe (so they can trade regularly), and that there is no impediment to trade from outsiders – that their markets are free and there is no exploitation.

This last is the answer to the false idea that men must be regulated to keep them from doing harm. In truth, there can be no general harm in a society based upon free choice and free trade. Overwhelmingly the vast majority of men make their own decisions, and this ensures that the vast majority of trades in society are beneficial.

The capitalist system helps men integrate the principles of morality with the principles of trade. Man learns to value his mind and its ability to think, to create values, and to trade with others. He builds his understanding upon an objective foundation that helps him or her stay grounded in reality. Reason teaches men how to think, how to conceptualize, how to act morally, and how to value life, liberty, and trade. Capitalist society regularizes cooperation, and this helps men build wealth. The convergence of mind, morality, and trade validates the role of the free mind in human survival.

This is where men learn that Marxism, communism, socialism, and fascism are based upon a philosophy of interference and exploitation. These societies regularize coercion and theft by introducing force as a constant. Force disrupts all of the benefits of capitalism and turns society into a wasteful exercise of financial disruption, over-regulation, and money laundering.

In order to have regularity in society, men must respect the sanctity of contract, trade, and property. In short, when men fight intervention into their trades, they are fighting against force in society. Interventionism is anti-capitalism. It pretends to save capitalism when, in fact, it is trying to disrupt the "regularity" of social and economic relationships among men. The advocates of small interventions promise to "fix" something they think is wrong in capitalism. In fact, fixing anything in capitalism is a false quest. The process of engaging in small interventions turns men from self-interest to sacrifice for the sake of the collective.

There is a great deal of equivocation today around the practice of interventionism. It starts with the hidden premise of an interventionist society, the use of the word "democracy" as a euphemism for "communism". When a leftist uses the term "democracy", he does not mean what most people take democracy to be. He does not mean a republic (that fosters self-rule through checks and balances) as it is known today. Rule by the majority (democracy), in the Greek sense, is rule of the crowd over the life and property of the individual. Rule by the majority is what communists mean when they defend democracy. In fact, communism is totalism, complete control by government over the lives of individuals. Totalism is the destruction of individual freedom and reason.

The Founding Fathers, as they deliberated about the society we would have, studied the "systems" of the past and sought to mitigate the influences of coercive factors in the societies of the past. They rejected rule by the majority as an oppressive and unfair (toward individuals) principle, and they elevated the concept of the rule of law. They sought a society that effectively outlawed coercion (on the part of government) and they developed a limited government to check the use of political power against individuals.

A limited government is constituted in such a way that it respects and protects the individual rights of citizens. For instance, the concept of separation of powers divides the separate branches of government into specific and delimited functions. These separate functions block each branch of government from exerting complete power without having a check in other branches. For instance, in our government, the executive branch implements the laws while the legislative branch writes and passes the laws (and directs expenditures). The last check is the responsibility of the judicial branch exclusively to interpret the laws according to the constitution that defines the rights of individuals.

Even more directly, the Bill of Rights in the constitution is a list of actions the government cannot take. For instance, the government cannot regulate speech, association, religion (ideas), and more. These restrictions on the government serve to protect freedom and the ability of people to live their lives morally. These restrictions, for the most part, influence the freedom of people to act economically. They collectively represent the concept of individual rights that are held by every individual in society. The judicial system should stand as the guardian of these principles, making judgment on government actions that violate individual rights.

Capitalism, because it is based upon individual rights, liberates men to act for their self-interest. It makes *acting* possible and this makes capitalism the greatest wealth-building economic system in history. Whenever capitalism is *practiced* in its pure unregulated form, it becomes the key to prosperity and human flourishing. Contrary to the views of anti-capitalists who claim that capitalism is anarchistic and chaotic, true capitalism creates the order in society that makes possible voluntary trade and contractual relationships.

Capitalism requires reason in decision-making. Reason (correct thinking) is the faculty that liberates man to act with decisiveness and efficiency. This is why capitalism is the only proper economic system. Reason leads to correct action while other systems are based upon emotional thinking.

Reason is not common today because of the advocacy of religion by many so-called capitalists. A morality based upon commandments does not give man a solid foundation for decisions that fall outside the realm the commandments. Despite this, most religious capitalists are able to separate their religious principles when it comes to economic thinking.

When a society rejects reason and capitalism, it tends to create destructive modes of morality. The logical fallacy of altruism moves men to think that self-sacrifice is the moral thing to do. Little do they realize that altruism, the giving up of values, actually destroys life because it destroys the motivation for moral action. The "giving up of values" in the society based upon sacrifice leads to self-destruction that, over time, destroys life and prosperity. This is because you can never have enough sacrificing in the altruist society. Whenever you spend stolen loot, the problems are still there, and they require more sacrificing that never solves the problems.

Individualism

In my book, Individualism, I wrote:

"Individualism is a view of life that identifies the proper role of the self in the universe. It postulates that the Individual is supremely important and that the Individual life is an end in itself.

"Do you want to live a better life? Do you want to be a better person? Do you want to enjoy yourself and understand that "living well" is not a bad thing? If you want this experience, then I suggest you keep reading. This book is about you and how you can get the most out of life. It seeks to help you understand your individuality as well as the obstacles to "living well" imposed by religion and modern philosophy.

"As long as man is man - as long as he has the capacity of reason - there will always reside within him a self. Though sometimes submerged beneath the terror and pretense that accompany modern society, the true self thinks about what it needs, not what others need, what it wants, not what others want, what it values, not what others value, seek or do.

"The opposite of Individualism is otherism. This view creates confusion, it asks for blind faith, gives magic, and miracles, and ghosts and demons. The self attempts to find understanding. Otherism creates self-doubt, and gives guilt, and scary masks (disapproving faces), prejudice and discrimination against the self. The self attempts to resolve doubt. Otherism fosters joining, and gives ritual, group activities, and mindless promiscuity (unconditional love toward all persons). Within this orgy of otherism, the self would rather be alone, or with another self that is admired.

"Yet, without a road map toward the self, the true self is lost and frustrated. He wants nothing more than happiness, repose and serenity. These are seemingly impossible, not because the Individual is incapable of finding them, but because the only solutions offered by culture are humiliatingly otherist—they promise happiness as a reward for being "good" according to their precepts – but they give and engender only humiliation. Little is said about obtaining happiness by thinking, by questioning, challenging the culture, challenging the very idea that happiness can be achieved by ritual joining. Rather, otherism offers collectivist ideas, groups to join, rituals to practice, self-sacrifice and self-abnegation.

"When I talk about successfully maintaining the Individual self, I am talking about an ideology or a set of ideas that, once accepted, makes one an Individualist. I am talking about something difficult to achieve: what one started with, the core of one's being, the integrity of one's soul. I am talking about being at one's core physically and mentally and functioning in such a way that one never betrays, through outside influences, the integrity of that core, the integrity of the self. I am talking about taking the self joyously and guarding the inviolability of that self.

"Notice that I did not say one should take oneself seriously. I said take the self "joyously." And indeed that is what one feels when one is happy about one's self. When one sees a happy, guiltless face, one that does not demand obedience and agreement, one that says, I am happy and I hope you are happy too; one is seeing a person living in his core. Taking one's self joyously means casting off the fire-ridden, hell-ridden, humility-ridden, slavery-ridden, sad and tortured traits that come when society tells us to take ourselves seriously.

"Joy is the successful state of life and it is joy that resides in the Individual who has earned his mind. The person who takes himself joyously has no fear, is serene in the recognition that he loves himself and those he has selected to receive the expression of his self-love. He takes himself joyously when he recognizes that his greatest asset is not just his happiness but also his mind. He recognizes that productivity is the expression of that joyous reliance on his mind and that it will enable him to become established in a proper society as a person who has earned respect from those around him. He gives life and enables life and nurtures life and loves life. He is moved by his joy which is an expression of the kind of person he has created. The battle of the Individual vs. the collective is the battle between joy for the Individual and terror of the crowd.

"A person who has succeeded in maintaining his Individual self detects very easily the person in the opposite state, the person who has strayed from his core and placed others at the center of his being. Such a person is obvious because of the pretenses that populate his facial structure, the fears that populate his musculature, the faked conviviality, the faked love, the faked concern, the phony smile, the habitual avoidance of life, the constant effort to in some way affect others.

"The Individualist may or may not be a brilliant genius. Intelligence is not a necessity for Individualism (although it helps). The Individualist has a source of knowledge few are able to engage: the integrity of the spirit, the ability to recognize what feels right (according to his values) and the strength not to be overwhelmed by the terrorizing of others. This integrity is part of each person when he starts out in life; and the key issue is the extent and degree to which he is able to maintain it. This adherence amounts to the subconscious statement: "I will do what I choose so long as it achieves my goals and expresses my happiness, my feeling of wellbeing, my sense of what is right for me as this right proceeds from my core, my fully integrated body."

"It is from this core that a philosophy, an ideology of Individualism, proceeds. The precepts of this philosophy state unequivocally that each man is a value in himself with inalienable rights not to be trampled by others, that the universe is open to man and his actions, that man can control his destiny, provided he also recognizes the inviolability of the rights of other human beings; and especially, so long as he pursues the highest thinking, his highest expression of reason as it informs his choices, values and purpose.

"The key requirement of Individualism is that each man know who he is, where he is and what he will do about it. He must know that he is free to pursue and achieve whatever his mind has decided he desires, and that there should be no impediment to this pursuit from any source, especially from within and especially from the thoughts, actions and ideologies of others.

"Individualism says more than "just be yourself." It says that as an Individual human being you are a rare and unique entity. It says that no one has the right to defile you, to suppress you, to manipulate you or to force you. It says that you have the right to blossom as the Individual you are, to pursue and achieve your potential. It says you have the right to do whatever your rational mind selects so long as that action does not violate the rights of others. It says that your freedom is yours--by right, not by privilege, not by the dispensation of a collective. It says that you can be different--that difference is what makes you what you are. More than this, it says that you have no choice about being different--you are already a unique Individual who must *learn* about your difference and its expression. It says that you are beautiful and that beauty, if allowed to flower will take you to heights of wonderment, joy and happiness, so long as you do not allow it to be tainted by otherism--the branding iron of which is made up of conformity and mediocrity and likeness and promiscuity.

" Individualism, above all, releases you to use your mind for the sake of your goals. It tells you that the use of your mind is the highest mark of an individual and that the "real" you is your most rational you. It tells you that truth is the ultimate standard and honesty is one of the highest virtues. It tells you that your mind is a tool capable of learning all that you need for survival, and that the mark of your individuality is how well you use it, and how well you protect it against the corruption of collectivism. Individualism is not the constant repetition of mindless rituals; it is living in the moment and identifying, not by the gut or instincts, but by the mind, what the moment requires for your life and goals. Individualism is having an active mind.

"Individualism is the only source of that one emotion that is the highest of all, love and reverence for the highest values as they are exemplified in the person one chooses. Individualism is the source of love. A deep abiding love, fidelity and devotion, are possible only by recognition of the individuality and uniqueness of another person. Such a love sweeps aside the collective mingling so common today. If one is in love, and it is a true love, then you know what I mean. Look at that love and see just how much Individualism is involved, notice that individuality is the source of the strength of your love and you will begin to know and understand just how evil is collectivism and how beautiful and peaceful life and society can be by the establishment of the ego."[7]

---

[7] Individualism by Robert Villegas Copyright 2015 by Robert Villegas

Also, from my book Individualism:

"Can a person be a collectivist by honest conviction? Or is there an element of dishonesty involved? It is certainly true that most of us are exposed to collectivism when we are very young, before we have the intellectual ammunition to fight back. It is also true that collectivist teachers expect blind acceptance of their ideas—that they consider collectivism good without question. This is because most of them have lost the ability to connect ideas to reality, and to recognize the very real consequences of those ideas.

"Still others look around and see the problems of the world and decide that collective action is the only way to solve those problems. They certainly care about others and want to be able to solve human problems. Their mistake is that they too easily compromise with a wide range of ideas that include collectivism and altruism. Rather than question these ideas they create their own version of "sanity" by combining love of humanity with collectivism, completely unaware that collectivism is actually hatred of humanity. This compromising view makes it impossible for them to recognize evil in the very ideas they hold so lovingly.

"As a youngster, I remember reading about an Indiana landmark called New Harmony, IN, a town founded on the principles of collectivism. I wondered how such a great idea could have failed and I sought to find out. I learned that the idea of collectivism in New Harmony had led to much resentment among the able people who found themselves overworked and underpaid. New Harmony had shown that the able resented having to work for those who did not work and as they began to leave the community, the town's great ideal of collectivism had collapsed.

"It took Ayn Rand, an Arch-Individualist, to explain that collectivism was not about helping the needy but about exploiting the able. During her time, the left controlled everything and, until reading Rand, I believed the lie that the Soviet Union would someday overcome the U.S.A. But if Rand was correct that collectivism is a war against the able, how could the Soviets have had a great economy? Certainly, the collapse that occurred in the society of New Harmony was happening in the Soviet Union too since the same principles were being enacted in both societies. I predicted, among my family and friends, that eventually the Soviet Union would collapse.

"Although some teachers and authority figures are dupes mouthing collectivist slogans because they have nothing original to say (a lifetime of repeating collectivist clichés has killed originality), political leaders must be feared and controlled--lest their power lust lose control, as with Hitler and Stalin. It is these types of people who are not innocent.

"On the other hand, there is some truth to the idea that teachers and authorities are willfully evading the devastation of collectivism. The history of the 20th Century is a testament to the devastating horror created by collectivism. In fact, most educators who deal with the subject are still baffled by the rise of Nazi Germany and can't pinpoint just what caused this lunacy. This is because there is so much collectivism in our culture that we have failed to realize that the atrocities before, during and after World War II, were caused by an adherence to collectivism.

"In the chapter, "Coming to Grips with Racism", I state that collectivism "was the scourge of the 20th Century and would devastate the 21st if not defeated as a philosophical and political ideal." This is quite a charge against an institution that is seen as benevolent and proper for man. In this chapter, I intend to investigate the very real differences between collectivism and Individualism in order to show that collectivism is indeed a scourge and that Individualism is the only hope.

"Most people today have never been explicitly confronted with the idea of collectivism. Most do not know that it is a political ideal used by some intellectuals to identify a movement whose goal is to mold men into docile slaves. Additionally, the idea that Individualism is a viable alternative to collectivism has seldom been discussed though it is crucial for the survival of our way of life. Indeed, most people have simply absorbed collectivism from their parents and teachers without even hearing the word "collectivism." Most believe that belonging to a group, participating in group activities and fostering group goals are good. Most, therefore, see group membership as a civilizing influence in man's history. Unwittingly, most of us are collectivists.

"Given the dominance of collectivism in our culture, does the absence of debate about its nature indicate a conspiracy of some sort? Are our cultural leaders attempting to pull a fast one, so to speak, on each generation, merely taking collectivism for granted without even offering a viable option? Is it possible that we have been duped about this important debate for centuries and that each of us has been thrust, without choice, into a collectivist universe? It would seem so.

"Indeed, the advocates of collectivism have never offered a viable justification for their views; we are seldom allowed to consider any alternatives to collectivism through an open dispassionate debate. Our educational system merely takes it for granted that it is good to find a group, that group loyalty is good, that groups of people getting together to help others is good, that joining a collective is a sure way to happiness. Indeed, the collectivists rule the day because they control the culture. Even in a society where freedom of speech is held in high regard, there are few that are openly advocating an alternative to collectivism.

"Rather, men are told that we must work together to solve social problems, that no man is an island, that men should help each other and that it is better to give than to receive. That collectivism has devastated more lives than egotistical capitalists has been ignored. That entrepreneurial capitalism has done more good worldwide than collectivist governmental bureaucracies is never acknowledged. That collectivism is responsible for most of the evil that humanity has brought into this world is a scandalous omission. Indeed, in a society of free speech and free inquiry, we have been forced by the authority of our educators to avoid investigation of the very real impact that collectivism has had on societies. We have been given, from our first days on earth, nothing less than glowing propaganda about the value of collective goals while we are enslaved for such goals that deliver none of the promised benefits.

"There are three possible ways a person can approach life: 1. Fear and capitulation to collectivism, 2. Fear and rebellion against the collective moral imperatives ("If this be evil, then make the most of it"), 3. Motivation by reason (Individualism).

"The last only leads to happiness. The others lead to neurosis and are the cause of most psychological problems.

"Man is a creature who evolved from an earlier animal that did not have the ability to use reason. Before man was man, he survived like other animals using automatic survival methods, such as pleasure/pain and fight/flight. These are what I call primitive survival devices.

"Yet, there are other devices designed to prepare the child for adulthood--I call them primitive teaching. One form of primitive teaching is done by the adult who serves as an example for the growing child. The adult, in effect, plays with the child, simulating the hunt, with the child the hunted and the adult the hunter. There is a built-in mechanism in the child to emulate or imitate the adult. This is called "acting-out." The child later does toward other creatures what is done toward him. This provides, in the wild, the ability to hunt and survive.

"Another form of primitive teaching is accomplished when the child observes the adult perform the actions that are required for survival. The child absorbs or incorporates the adult's behavior and begins to "practice" the survival method in preparation for adulthood.

"These primitive teaching devices can be observed in many animal species, especially mammals. What is critical for our purposes is to recognize that these mechanisms are still within man. They are still functioning. Treat a child in a certain way and he will treat others in the same way. Act in a certain way and the child will imitate those actions.

"Why do I call these primitive devices? They are primitive because they evolved at a time when man's mind was not capable of abstract thinking; was not capable of rationally deciding what to do. They worked perfectly well for the survival of the species, but like all primitive methods they were not perfect. Sometimes the opposite of survival took place as happens today when an animal drinks poisoned water or runs out in front of an automobile thinking the car is a large creature invading territory.

"Man, unlike all other creatures, developed reason, and it was reason that made "acting-out" behaviors obsolete. Reason was able to distinguish truths and facts to help him understand the rules of nature. Reason enabled man to change habits by formulating and acting upon new knowledge. And it was the process of abstracting concepts such as quality and quantity that helped create knowledge. Man also recorded facts and ideas to pass to future generations. Reason helped man develop technology, hence the evolution into "Technological Man." Reason was a better way.

"Why is this important for our understanding of the treatment of individuals? Reason is an attribute of the individual. It is a chosen activity that must be engaged by each child. And more importantly, we now have the requirement as adults, not to teach children to merely imitate and "act-out," but to teach them how to think. And it is this responsibility that, above all, is the one responsibility collectivists have encouraged us to ignore.

"If you analyze primitive societies, you will notice that they characteristically handle their children by teaching them to "act-out" and imitate. This is what makes them primitive. This is why their technology is primitive. This is why they are steeped in mysticism and mythology that carry from generation to generation unchanged. The primitive, ritualistic society is the closest that man can come to his animal nature.

"Through modern philosophy, in spite of our ability to use reason, our culture has brought into today's society all the premises of the ritualistic mentality: collectivism, mysticism, altruism, fear, acting-out and imitation. "Give a modern child these concepts and you destroy his ability to reason, his ability to be man. The more seriously he takes you the more animal-like he becomes. Most psychological problems today are an outgrowth of the stunting of the ability to reason inflicted on the Individual by poor parenting, bad school teachers, dogmatic churches, overbearing authority figures and cruel peers – all given power by collectivism.

"Look at the children that some parents create, the gangsters, the mindless thugs, the drooling illiterates that populate our popular culture and you can see the victory of collectivism. This is the visible product of collectivism precisely because collectivism cannot hold reason as a value. Reason contradicts faith and it is faith that collectivism fosters. A man of faith is an unquestioning man that can be controlled and who will do what he is taught to do—he is a man who will act out the ritual wars of the collectivist culture. Faith, to the collectivist propagandist is superior to reason in spite of the fact that none has been able to show how a man operating from faith and fear is superior.

"The visible product of collectivist primitivism is everywhere around us, and has not, until now, been identified because, much like primitive tribes, we find ourselves engaged in "we" thinking and don't realize that what we take for granted as necessary for survival is precisely what is making our survival difficult. Did we realize that this orgy of criminality and commonality in our neighborhoods was nothing more than our children acting-out what they saw us do or say? Did we realize that their gangsterism was the product of one of our most basic cultural premises: collectivism? We look at today's social problems and tell ourselves we need more collectivism. When we ask ourselves, what has gone wrong in our society, have we looked at what we consider our highest value, our most dominant institution: collectivism? We tell ourselves that to deal with crime we need more collectivism-that the misguided youth has just chosen the wrong group. Instead of choosing his street gang, we exhort him to choose his church, or his family, or his tribe as his gang. We have always sought to find the negative premises that could create the mindless subculture that is responsible for this orgy of decline--and we cannot seem to understand the cause. The cause is our everyday thoughts and institutions as they are found in our philosophy books and comic books, in our movies and DVDs, in our prayer books and popular novels. These children are only imitating what they see. As we grope in confusion and helplessness to stop the trend toward social decline, we tell ourselves that we need more of the poison that is causing the decline. That poison is collectivism."[8]

Full collectivism is communism. I call communism totalism. When you advocate for the idea of government providing full medical care, full income re-distribution, full senior care, full childhood care services, anything that is needed, you are advocating communism. To date, would-be communists have advocated incrementalism, smaller coercive programs that were designed to smuggle communism into society; while today leftists, so far, are not totalists. This is what a totalist would say:

---

[8] Individualism by Robert Villegas Copyright 2015 by Robert Villegas

"I just have to remind you. Don't you ever let anybody take your power from you. You have the same power that you did before November 5th, and you have the same purpose that you did. And you have the same ability to engage and inspire. So don't ever let anybody or any circumstance take your power from you."[9]

Although the Democrats lost power in the last election Harris is declaring that her supporters should assume that they still have the total power they thought they had before their loss. The implication is that they should assume the power of total control of society regardless of the perception that they have been repudiated. This is cognitively the biggest mistake they should make – that they should assume that they still control events in society and that they should falsely assume that they still have that control. This is because, as moral totalists, as altruists, they should assume that they have the moral power and responsibility to rule society. This is full arrogance.

---

[9] Kamala Harris YouTube video.

Today, capitalism is unappreciated around the world. This is because of the influence of the morality of altruism. Altruism justifies the expropriation of property and wealth for the sake of "giving" benefits to those who have not earned wealth, as well as those who earn wealth only through government assistance or aid programs. In fact, much of the money from aid programs is laundered from tax dollars to fraudulent uses.

The proponents of altruism argue that re-distribution of income is beneficial to society in general while they ignore the harm to those tax payers who are forced to give up their values. To the extent that a society is heavily regulated (a process called interventionism), re-distribution, in its various forms, causes the economy to be sluggish and inefficient. If men were to recognize the validity of individual rights, that these rights should never be violated, then they would be able to throw off government intervention in society.

In my book, *"The History of Altruism"*, in the chapter "Dissecting Altruism, I wrote:

"Before we can understand an idea such as altruism, we must give its advocates the floor. We must let them make their case and then we can proceed to dissect the idea to determine if the advocates are correct or whether they are lying to us.

"Altruism starts with a smile from its advocates. The altruist must first convince you that he, himself, is a good man, a kind man, a lover of men. He must put you at ease and assure you that he only seeks what is best for man.

"Yet, you must wonder; why the smile? Why the need to assure you that he is a good person? This is because he must convince you that the outcome of an altruistic act is good and his smile is his judgment of himself as good, and from this, he can take the leap to the idea that if he, a good man, is going to convince you that the results of altruism are good, then you must trust him.

"This is because there is no verifiable proof that altruism actually brings about good. This means that the altruist must bring with him a level of authority before he can convince you he is good, and that altruism brings good about. The smile is the beginning of that authority, but the top level of that authority, higher up, is the authority of God.

"What is God? God is, to the altruist, the ultimate authority on the nature of the good. God is the source of all good and so altruism, if it is to be accomplished, must be based upon the ultimate good; and for many people, that ultimate good must be something spiritual, non-existent, and ephemeral. Metaphysical dualism informs them that the spiritual world is superior, so if God says that man should make the ultimate sacrifice for others, then there is no doubt that God is ultimately correct.

"I suggest we dig a little deeper. To accept a spiritual answer to our moral questions is to remove ourselves from existence, reality. A spiritual answer is essentially a logical leap, a movement from uncertainty to moral certainly without an examination of cause and effect. The result is an ultimate sacrifice that is not justified by the facts. We need a secular answer to the question about the value of altruism.

"When we accept a "spiritual" truth without an intervening logical process, we inevitably will make the wrong act. For instance, let's assume you have worked hard all your life to create values that you trade with others. This process of value creation brings to you the benefits associated with working hard, money, leisure, comfort, pride and a precise value that you have striven for and achieved through logical thinking and reasonable action. Your life is improved and you can prove it by reference to reality, your bank account, your home, your leisure, your happiness.

"Then, here comes the altruist to tell you that you owe your values to people who did not use the same precision of thought, the deliberative action and did not create their values for themselves. The altruist tells you that you must now disrupt your chosen goals, give them up to someone who did not engage in the demanding thought you engaged in and that it is a matter of right that you should sacrifice the work of your lifetime to a person who did not engage in exacting thought for himself. Is it not an injustice to demand sacrifice from you? Are you not losing in this sacrifice? Are you not proving to the other person that he need not engage in goal-directed action, but you should? The only answer to your questions is "God wills it and you cannot question the demands of duty to your fellow man".

"But you ask, where is God's logical process? Where is the reason in demanding that you give up your values? If you point to real damage to your life, real disruption of your thought and hard work, a distortion of what people call moral living, there is no answer. Your goal is to live for others, and you cannot shirk this responsibility. In fact, the cruelty of demanding your values has become their cry that it is you who is cruel in refusing those demands. How can you live under such rules of morality? It is clear that your moral living has enabled his immoral living.[10]

"Let's look at a real-life example:

"If I were to tell you about a previous robbery I had witnessed, I would give you all the details, the location, day, time and especially the name of the individual who had been robbed. But what would have been particularly important to mention is how much harm and loss the robbery had done to the person who had been robbed.

---

[10] "Kant's analysis of the common moral concepts of "duty" and "good will" led him to believe that we are free and autonomous as long as morality, itself, is not an illusion. Yet in the *Critique of Pure Reason*, Kant also tried to show that every event has a cause. Kant recognized that there seems to be a deep tension between these two claims: If causal determinism is true then, it seems, we cannot have the kind of freedom that morality presupposes, which is "a kind of causality" that "can be active, independently of alien causes *determining* it" (G 4:446).

"Kant thought that the only way to resolve this apparent conflict is to distinguish between *phenomena*, which is what we know through experience, and *noumena*, which we can consistently think but not know through experience. Our knowledge and understanding of the empirical world, Kant argued, can only arise within the limits of our perceptual and cognitive powers. We should not assume, however, that we know all that may be true about "things in themselves," although we lack the "intellectual intuition" that would be needed to learn about such things.

"These distinctions, according to Kant, allow us to resolve the "antinomy" about free will by interpreting the "thesis" that free will is possible as about noumena and the "antithesis" that every event has a cause as about phenomena. Morality thus presupposes that agents, in an incomprehensible "intelligible world," are able to make things happen by their own free choices in a "sensible world" in which causal determinism is true." - Kant's Moral Philosophy, *First published Mon Feb 23, 2004; substantive revision Fri Jan 21, 2022, Stanford Encyclopedia - Kant's Moral Philosophy (Stanford Encyclopedia of Philosophy)*

"You'd want to know whether there had been a struggle, a beating or whether the victim had been seriously harmed or even killed? Indeed, most of our focus would have been on the terrible harm that had come to the victim. This is as it should be. A robbery is a serious violation of an individual's right to his life and property. A robbery is an evil act; it is the forcible taking of value from one person by someone who did not deserve what he had taken.

"But if I were to discuss with you another event that involved an equally harmful act, you'd not even be concerned about the harm done to the victim. This act would have been done without the victim's consent; he would not even have been informed of it. This would have been the act of raising someone's taxes to pay for a new poverty program. With this event, we would not have thought that a crime had been committed. We would not even look at the victim here; instead, we'd look at the benefits that the beneficiary would be obtaining through the new program that had taken money from a productive individual. Yet, the same amount of money was taken from the victim of higher taxes as was taken from the robbery victim and the same amount of harm was done as well to both robbery victim and taxpayer.

"The difference is that the first act was a crime and the second was an act of altruism. Why the double standard here? What causes us to bemoan the loss of the robbery in one case and not even think about the loss in the case of altruism? This is a very important question because it gets to the heart of a pervasive blindness that infects our entire society; a cognitive blind spot created by the idea that giving money to the poor does no harm to the person providing the money.

"Essentially, there are three parties who participate in any act of altruism. I call it a transaction because value and money is transferred from the first party through the second party and to the third party.

"By contrast, a free transaction, one which is voluntary, does not have a middleman. Its intent is to create a win/win for both parties. And this happens millions of times a day which is one reason why economic freedom achieves affluence.

"The first party in an altruistic transaction is the **producer**, the person who must sacrifice for others. This person has something of value, either money, products, knowledge, intelligence or his own physical energy and time. The second party is the **moral authority**, the person who has the ability to direct the first person to give up something of value for the third person, the so-called **victim** whose condition supposedly requires that someone sacrifice for his/her sake.

"The Producer

"The producer is most often split between two moral codes. One code holds that he has a right to the pursuit of happiness and that self-sufficiency is the hallmark of a moral person. He plans his life in advance and decides how much he must produce in order to live the life he wants. This calculation is precise and adequate for the goal he has set. He believes in work and making his own way and he thinks that his value lies in his ability to create or make things.

"This code of self-sufficiency is contradicted by another code imposed upon him by the moral authority (society or religion) who tells him that his purpose in life is to relieve the suffering of the people who have supposedly been made poor by his pursuit of happiness. The moral authority has no consideration of the fact that, in forcing the producer to give, he has upset his plans for life; he has diminished his returns and forced him to recalculate the additional effort and time it will take him to reach his goals. For the moral authority, this negative consequence is unimportant. He thinks the producer can just pick up (producing) what he lost through a little more effort. No problem, he thinks. (parenthesis mine)

"Using the moral code of altruism, the moral authority promises different forms of punishment if the producer does not give up his time, energy or production for the sake of the victim. He will either be ostracized on earth as selfish (guilted) or he will suffer in eternity for his pride and lust (damned).

"Guilt and damnation imposed by the moral authority on the producer are often so strongly expressed that few producers can bear the onslaught of hatred and animosity extended toward them. Most producers, especially the most productive, do whatever is necessary to satisfy the demands of the moral authority because they are afraid that he might be right about their moral status. In fact, the producer, because he is often attacked in this way, spends his life fearing the ire of others, refuses to think for himself and settles for paying bribes to the moral authority and the victim. His goal becomes to prove that he is not the evil monster they claim he is. The psychological consequence for the producer, when he is insulted for being selfish, is to freeze morally, to be totally disarmed because he has accepted the moral authority's philosophy without question (For examples, see Gates and Buffet).

"The altruist morality holds that man's capacity for happiness is proof of his evil; it turns each man into his own worst enemy, his own accuser within the quiet reaches of his subconscious mind. The self-esteem he does not have, the normal acts he is not allowed to commit, the freedom he does not possess, give him only hatred of life and a jealous anger at other men who are not attacked in this way. Altruism kills self-sufficiency, pride and innocence, the very virtues that men need in order to be happy.

"Because the producer becomes morally frozen by the attacks of the moral authority, he is the ready target of anyone who would seek to exploit his thought, time and energy for his own benefit. All anyone has to do is tell him what they want, and he'll provide it; hoping that his acquiescence gains approval.

"There is only one solution to this loss of self-esteem. The statement he should utter is: "Enough. I have done nothing wrong. I will sacrifice no more."

"The Moral Authority

"The moral authority, has preached the philosophy of altruism for centuries. His goal is to convince the producer that he has a moral obligation, first, to accept his authority, and secondly, to do as he is told. More importantly, his goal is to manipulate the producer into a position of slavery and eventually to cause him to suffer. To accomplish this goal, he preaches that man is basically imperfect or evil, that his sin consists of pride and independence. He preaches the value of collective joining and attempts to convince the producer that "no man is an island", and that he, the producer, is worthless.

"There are basically two types of moral authority. The first type is the mystic who uses fear of "the ineffable" to cause people to lose confidence in their thinking abilities and to accept magic, miracles and "revelations" from God. He demands faith because he isn't sure he knows what he's talking about; and without faith, he would not be able to fill the producer's and the victim's minds with the philosophy of sacrifice.

"The second type of moral authority is the brutish politician or general who uses force and the threat of force to cause fear in people. He is also a mystic because he has no clue what goes on in the minds of the people he seeks to enslave and he knows that without force, no one will go along with his mindless lust for power. Sometimes, the mystic and the brute work together in plundering the productive people they enslave. Both need to reduce people to the status of unthinking slaves who will do whatever is demanded of them.[11]

"Both types of moral authority send out their "moral police" among society to ensure that everyone is sacrificing sufficiently. If you have ever criticized a young person for being too prideful, too happy, too selfish, too bright or too beautiful, then you have been an oppressive moral policeman.

"Every action engaged in by a human being has a moral meaning and a consequence. Naturally, that consequence should proceed from the nature of the act. However, since the moral authority has a corner on judgment and can interfere without any consequence, he is able to manipulate rewards to accomplish his own goals. He is, in a sense, a moral interventionist. This is because he has manipulated society into allowing him to dispense moral judgment and reward and punish action based upon his own standards rather than on the standards of the actor. Altruism, because it is a system that "adjusts" due rewards, necessarily creates injustice.

""Through injustice, a person can deflect or mute the natural consequences of another's actions. He can make one person's virtue pay for another's vice, for instance, by retaining a worker who performs poorly,

---

[11] For a full description of these types see "For the New Intellectual, the Philosophy of Ayn Rand"

and piling his ill-completed work onto more productive employees. He thereby prevents the good worker's virtue from achieving its natural reward and the poor worker from receiving his natural punishment. Similarly, the teacher who indiscriminately awards Bs to strong and weak essays alike deprives the worthy of the reward they have earned and bestows benefits on students who have not earned them."[12]

"The key to identifying the moral authority and his moral police are statements that reveal a negative moral evaluation of the producer. They also advocate government re-distribution programs to be paid for by the producer. Tell-tale statements include: "I have no problem with..." and finishing the statement with a coercive measure as if *his* "having no problem" with government enforced morality somehow wipes out the opinion of people who do have a problem with it. A common question is "Are we going to be the kind of society that..." then finishing the question with a supposedly benevolent goal that requires coercive measures, as if *his* deciding on the benevolent goal is a convincing argument against those who don't think it is benevolent at all. That some people disagree with him is of no consequence

---

[12] Ayn Rand's Normative Ethics by Dr. Tara Smith, Cambridge Paperback, page 144

to him since he has no problem with using force against people. Force is the great equalizer of men for the vicious moral authority. "Equity" is the goal of forceful manipulations. The end justifies the means. Injustice is the means toward the goal of equity.

""Suppose that, instead of evaluating individuals objectively and rewarding or punishing them as they deserve, we substituted some alternative standards: treating individuals as they asked to be treated, for instance, or as they needed, or as a democratic vote prescribed. The result would be to make life more difficult for the virtuous and more easy for the vicious. Whenever rewarding the life-furthering conduct or character of other individuals would not satisfy the substituted criterion of justice, the natural effects of those persons' actions would be thwarted. When we pass over the productive worker in order to supply the needier with a job, the productive worker is denied the logical results of his good work and we are all deprived of the further benefits likely to be gained from his receiving that reward. When we promote a person on the basis of his popularity rather than his performance, we can expect the same sort of losses. Such policies would stifle the stream of values that virtue typically generates. While many would recognize this as unfair to the immediate recipients of such treatment, my point

here is that it makes life harder for everyone. Failing
to treat individuals as they deserve works against the
demands of human survival."[13]

"The influence of modern philosophy in society
makes it appear that the moral authority is invisible
in human transactions. This is because people are
educated, by altruist propaganda, to "voluntarily"
sacrifice in every situation. This "influence" is so
strong that many people are not able to develop
other means of interaction that do not include or
require altruism. The moral authority uses powerful
examples of the altruistic premise in order to
convince people that sacrifice is the proper thing to
do in all circumstances. This makes altruism into a
powerful motivating factor in society, so powerful
that most people naturally think altruistic thoughts
as a matter of course. They are afraid that the
altruist's "evil eye" will catch them in the act of being
selfish. That's why they call it "self"-sacrifice.
Altruism and the injustice practiced by the moral
authority are the modern equivalents of "ritual"
human sacrifice led by the witch doctor of primordial
times. The witch doctor equals the moral authority.

"The Victim

---

[13] Ibid, page 146-147

"It should be clear by now that altruism, the sacrifice of the good for the evil, represents a reversal of the concept of justice through which the producer and the victim have switched places. The victim is any non-entity whose lack of education, initiative or values has rendered him helpless in the work of survival. He is a victim of the moral authority, who has taught him to be passive and who has coddled him into believing that some harm has been done to him by the producer. The method of injustice imposed upon the producer has become the argument for "justice" on behalf of the victim. This moral inversion results in the obliteration of the relationship between the cause of production and the effect of plunder. The mind produces but the gun disposes.

"A key characteristic of the presumed victim, and in particular, a key to understanding him or her is to recognize, not only his physical need of the producer, but his need of other people to affect his survival. The victim is taught that he cannot survive without others, and this motivates him to enlist others to help him, and more importantly, to love him. He feigns innocence, ignorance, weakness, and subservience in order to elicit from others a feeling of empathy and pity. The victim needs others, can't live without others, not in order to provide for them, but to have them provide for him. The victim must, as a matter of survival, become pathetic. Not only is the victim a loser in life, but he pretends that it isn't his fault.

"There is something that both the producer and the victim have in common. They are both taught that they are deficient. The victim is told that he cannot survive on his own and the producer is told that he is the cause of the plight of the victim. Both are being lied to and this is particularly visible when one of the victims decides to educate himself and become a producer. He will most often be strongly discouraged from doing so.

"One thing you will seldom see is the moral authority going to peoples' homes to ask them if they need something from government. The result is that many poor people languish, believing the propaganda of altruism, but wondering also what to do – since no one has come to help. Eventually, they learn that in order to obtain the benefits of government, they will have to "apply" (beg) for them. This often involves standing in line in a dingy government building, looking at the uncaring faces of people who can't be fired from their jobs, filling out forms and then being rejected by letter. Then they must go back to the government office in order to appeal (beg some more), stand in line again and be told they have to fill out more paperwork. In time, their careers become standing in line for benefits. The only real enjoyment they get is being able to watch television at the government office and to hear from the moral authority how lucky they are that he loves them.

"Yet, the key for understanding altruism is that there are not enough producers to take care of the growing number of victims. This means it is not possible for the moral authority to collect enough funds for the victim to be taken care of. So, the victim usually languishes in poverty as he waits for the next government program to be created. His life becomes a drudgery as he subconsciously feels guilty for being lazy and not taking care of himself.

"This creates the call for "full" communism where all income is confiscated and re-distributed to all people. This gives the moral authority unlimited power over a diminishing return. The result is the Soviet Union, secret police, labor unions and social destruction as in Venezuela."[14]

As a good altruist, you are expected to control and restrict your pride, not to mention your striving for excellence. You are taught to subconsciously give up your values for others. You are supposed to become angry at people who express pride and self-interest

---

[14] The History of Altruism by Robert Villegas

under the assumption that these moral concepts are evil. In fact, when you see people being "sinful" (when they think for themselves), you should put on a metaphorical angry mask and aim it toward them and to make them afraid of your moral judgment of them for being so bad as to be free in action because you are not a good altruist.

On the other hand, self-interested people are exposed by the Marxists to anger and manipulation and made to feel guilty for self-reliance and self-interest. They expect people to allow their exploitation and consider the angry attitudes of the altruists to be a form of the good. This last is the premise that people should challenge if they are to recover their innocence and freedom.

In my book entitled "Behind the Ritual Mask", I wrote:

"Before Greek drama, there were the passion plays and initiation rites of the Mystery religions. These passion plays were a reenactment of myth where the initiate was a participant in the drama involving the life of the deity. The initiate was a member of the host of humanity who must purify himself, reach catharsis, and find a new more pure understanding of man's role in life through the adventures of Dionysus and other Promethean-like figures. Catharsis meant a new understanding, a seeing of the light and an elevated knowledge of the deeper meanings of the Mystery religions.

"The Greeks feared the mob because their society was partly an outgrowth of terror and of experimentation with both collectivist and legally constituted society. This is seen in their most important myths, the Iliad and the Odyssey where the gods interfered in human affairs on a regular basis. Their collective was a symbol of the irrationality and pettiness of their gods not to mention their utter disregard for mere men. As the gods go, so do men. As above, so below. This is the principle of religious emulation and the Greeks were very religious in this regard. They, their chorus and their collective danced the ritual dance of hatred of the ego, the melding into society of the mystery religions, of punishment of anyone who had the effrontery to be like god."[15]

"The ancient myths of religion ignore, and depend upon, the fact that man is a creature who chooses values, and those values are required for both survival and pleasure. In fact, the rituals based upon the religious cultural paradigms discussed in this book limit man's choices and pleasures, restrict his actions to a small range of pre-approved activities and make him into a creature of intellectual laziness and moral compromise – an actor in a play reciting lines. They represent merely the actions and pleasures that authority figures allow to man so they can control his mind and his pleasures – leaving the broad range that would normally have been available through reason as forbidden. "Their methods of control consign man to a dark tunnel of repetition and sameness, make him a creature limited only to a small part of his truth, with only one path available that yields a false understanding of himself as an automaton, without choice except to choose the prescribed, forbidden to go beyond the myth, forbidden to leave the cage that he has learned to love.

"As we noted above, the earliest forms of ritual about which we know were the ritual dances of the passion plays and Greek drama. In each story, there were always lessons learned about life, love and the

---

[15] Behind the Ritual Mask by Robert Villegas https://amzn.to/4gfjQSi

perennial struggle between good and evil as well as man's role in the universe. The struggle between good and evil was seen by early man as central to life and morality, a struggle in which man must participate in an effort to rid the world of the evil, both through his own acts of kindness and by battling the evil people who represented infidels/pagans.

"Ritual had the following purposes in ancient cultures, 1) to appease the gods, 2) to express or internalize the basic premises that are embedded in the culture in order to make them habit, 3) to achieve catharsis in the initiate, 4) to advance collective social or cultural goals and 5) to enable the individual to self-objectify through enactment of a prescribed role and thereby experience a sense of moral belonging to a group through repetition of easily performed and culturally approved acts.

"What characterizes mythical stories is that man in those stories is fated to suffer and die as both a pawn of destiny and as a stand in for the suffering god. Why such myths required suffering, pain, unhappiness, is a matter for conjecture, but it is safe to say, that the ancients were influenced in this direction by their own ideas of a malevolent and harsh environment that contained massive storms, floods, earthquakes, volcanic eruptions, etc., presumably brought to man as punishment for a variety of human flaws. To the ancients, man could only be saved from the wrath of the gods, through obedience, propitiation, emulation and eventually by becoming one with the gods through a supreme sacrifice (the ancient source of today's altruism). (parenthesis mine)

"A major contradiction in ritualism is that a ritualized person equates "must do" with "it is right to do." He is taught that cultural authorities know more than he knows and therefore what they preach *must* be right. This explains why so many of the things people do regularly are a chore and why so many people hate their lives and work. They are doing only what they are supposed to do in the face of a social response that criticizes them if they stray from the ritualized behavior. They do "what is right," (what they must do) receiving little pleasure from it and they avoid doing what they want to do in order to avoid hatred.

"Consider the implications of the following: if much of what religious people do is ritual, such as going to church, criticizing and punishing their children for being prideful, then they have lost the fundamental (reality-based) reasons why they do many things. Needless to say, with some of the most common habits, it takes merely a moment's reflection to identify the 'reason' why they do them, but if they avoid doing things they want because of fear of hatred, then they have only one motive in life (whether they know it or not): to compromise with the collective. Further, when everything they do is done because it must be done, then they have little to think about, they need only repeat in action what they "know" they must do. This approach gives them little to enrich their lives except the "enrichment" found in obedience and compromise. If an individual avoids doing some things out of fear of hatred, what does that make of his life except that he is dominated and controlled by fear?

"This situation points to the utter irresponsibility of our cultural leaders in blindly passing on outdated and illogical cultural paradigms and feeding them to young people without analysis and validation. The young child, looking for acceptance and understanding, has no way of knowing that the influences thrust upon him are deadly and dangerous. He becomes an actor on a stage, repeating the same rituals, in different forms, that were repeated in prehistoric mystery religions. But more importantly, he is taught, wrongly, that in order to obtain franchise in the world of humanity, he has to do and think in lock-step with the ideas given to him by the culture. He is taught that his value is created by their opinion of his willingness to live according to the dominant cultural paradigms of his age. Under this false premise, only altruism is culturally viable.

"Because the young individual is, for the most part, a blank slate, it is easy for him to accept the wrong ideas imposed by culture. Does anyone tell him that he is becoming a phony? No, they encourage his self-sacrificial behavior. Yet the desire to obtain the love of others through altruism is a "bait and switch." They convince him, or he assumes, that if he does "altruism" he will be loved. The switch comes when they tell him there is no reward; that the ritual of sacrifice is an end in itself, that he hasn't done enough of it, and that others are more important than he – which is in fact the original position that caused his self-doubt."[16]

One of the factors that keeps altruism influencing society is what I discussed above; the cathartic influence of altruism in society. Catharsis is defined by Oxford Languages as "providing psychological relief through the open expression of strong emotions." Catharsis, the Greek concept, is derived from the emotions deftly engendered by ancient Greek playwrights as they competed for literary prizes among Greek audiences. Catharsis led to emotional reactions that came out of the actions of the Greek gods. Yet, the role of catharsis in human life is much more widespread than we might think. In fact, catharsis has a heavy impact on human living; it stands as a hidden influence on life and living.

For example, the field of the creative arts, theater, literature, movies, video, etc. are all infused with cathartic factors, so much so that they cannot today

---

[16] Ibid

exist without them. Indeed, catharsis, based upon ritual, faith, and the lives of the gods, is a false quest. This is because it is dependent upon the misperception of the priests and other authoritarians.

Catharsis, connected to altruism, creates a cognitive error regarding the efficacy of altruism or lack thereof. When a false idea is taken as fundamental to human living, man's mind is given up to the demands for sacrifice in action. Catharsis is anti-thetical to reason and destroys morality in action. Men easily give up reason while holding sacrifice to be reasonable. The result is economic depression and the destruction of morality.

Today, our society, is a mixed economy, a mixture of regulations versus freedom, or, put another way, a society of force versus freedom. Interventions in the economy, by government, work to stifle free trade and create disruptions of trade. Despite the fact that altruism causes failure in society, people fall for the notion (propaganda) that government programs and large expenditures will provide major benefits. With starry eyes, they jump headlong to impose altruism by force, completely oblivious to the fact that they are violating the rights of individuals. In practice, this means that whenever sacrificial programs are proposed, people emotionally jump on the idea as a sensational "new" idea that will create abundance and prosperity. Nothing can be further from the truth.

The presidential candidacy of Donald Trump (in 2024) was conducted virtually without mention of the words "capitalism" or "free trade". Trump has shown himself to be an advocate of various forms of interventionism while many think he is a capitalist. His advocacy of tariffs and his inconsistent economic ideas indicate that he doesn't understand capitalism and its true benefits. As a "deal maker" he will work within the interventionist state while threatening policies that harm foreign trading partners. It is hard to say how much impact these interventions will have on our economy compared to his other more free market policies. I wonder if his tariffs will lead to wars or economic depression.

Trump and his administration represent a mixed bag of diverse economic and moral principles, and it is difficult to say how things will turn out. The only good thing to come out of his electoral victory is that the "totalism" (Marxism) of the left has been totally repudiated by the voters. In fact, this election of Trump leaves the philosophy of the left bereft of good ideas. The left has been reduced to name calling, gaslighting, lying, money laundering, bribery, lawfare, extortion, and people-trafficking. Nobody believes them when they promise to bring about a great society.

Virtually every economic system except capitalism produces failure. Fascism, socialism, communism, monarchy, each in their various forms, promise to re-distribute money and economic power, and *this* is why they always fail. The more such systems interfere with human trades, the more damage they do. Capitalism never fails while authoritarian systems always fail. Until and unless men learn that altruistic human sacrifice is an evil moral practice, they will never learn that capitalism is the greatest economic system in human history.

On the other hand, what I call totalism (a euphemism for Marxism), as it exists within the minds of the pragmatists in society, is to create hatred of capitalism through the invocations of "class struggles". Their answer to capitalism is the projection of altruism (false charity, re-distribution, and massive spending programs) and making it into a cathartic act and moral superiority. Altruism is an idea that will soon die, and the world will be better for it.

Yet, we must ask, "what is it about totalism and altruism that are supposed to inspire people?" The answer is cathartic self-sacrifice (duty). People are supposed to be inspired whenever progressives and religionists invoke self-sacrifice. Yet, people have gotten past the idea of self-sacrifice because they are starting to become aware that altruism is a proxy for theft and money laundering. People are no longer inspired by the aura of cathartically-induced "goodness" in altruism that was once supposed to inspire them to give up their values. In fact, they are starting to realize that Obama's "call to sacrifice" is actually the call for exploitation.

In fact, today's Marxist professors use lies to capture the human mind. Most people are jaded by the constant invocation of lies while others don't yet know they are being lied to. This last group can't recognize when Marxist divisions rear their lion's heads to consume them. In fact, Marxist lies have evolved into a cult of mind destruction in the name of saving knowledge and capitalism. This is why equivocation and adjective-switching are so common among the Marxists. They are literally programming our children to hate anything related to capitalism and the morality (individualism) that is good for the individual.

Yet not all is right on the right. There are the religious conservatives, most of whom care not a whit about capitalism. Instead, they are advocates of theocracy.

In my book, *The Conservative's Dilemna*, I wrote:

"I've enjoyed reading the books of Thomas Sowell for many years. I became aware of him in the late 1970s when he burst onto the intellectual scene with amazing analyses of economic trends. His defense of free markets is laudable and he has made many unique and perceptive contributions to our national political debate. Most recently he has written books that have been critical of intellectuals. I just finished one book that brought home to me the problem for conservatives and, especially, why they have found themselves on the losing end of the political debate.

"The book, entitled "Intellectuals and Society" is an excellent examination of progressive intellectuals' inability to bridge the gap between their elitist ideas and reality. The first few chapters of the book give an excellent overview of the problems that progressive intellectuals create. According to Professor Sowell, intellectuals are wrong about social solutions because they come at problems from a limited elitist perspective that represents only a small percentage of the total knowledge available in society at large.

"I find Doctor Sowell's criticism to be excellent when it comes to analyzing the precarious position of intellectuals who are steeped in specialized knowledge but who have little understanding of the real world. Yet his argument fell apart for me when he compared today's progressives with today's conservatives.

""[Their] vision of society, in which there are many "problems" to be "solved" by applying the ideas of morally anointed intellectual elites is by no means the only vision, however much that vision may be prevalent among today's intellectuals. A conflicting vision has co-existed for centuries—a vision in which the inherent flaws of human beings are the fundamental problem and social contrivances are simply imperfect means of trying to cope with that problem—these imperfections themselves being products of the inherent shortcomings of human beings."[17] (Brackets mine)

"Professor Sowell takes for himself the position of the conflicting vision. His preferred vision of man is "...the tragic vision of the human condition that is very different from the (left's) vision of the anointed."[18] And, indeed, he joins a long tradition of philosophers and intellectuals who have shared that vision of human beings as inherently flawed. Unfortunately, a fact that he seems to have missed is that this tragic vision of man is also held by the progressives.

---

[17] Intellectuals and Society, Thomas Sowell, Basic Books, hardcover page 77
[18] Ibid Page 77

"I wonder what he would say if I pointed out that the exalted view that intellectuals hold of *themselves* is not the same view they have of *man*. Their view of man derives from philosophers such as Kant, Hume and Marx that see men as intellectually incompetent, bereft of the ability to understand reality or the victims of economic factors outside of their control. None of those could be considered an exalted view of man. (Italics mine)

"You have to ask yourself what is the point of taking the position that man is inherently flawed? Why would conservatives want to start with this premise? And more importantly, why do they think that this position provides a better argument for limited government and capitalism?

"As a former Catholic, I am familiar with this view. According to the Church, man is a sinner who would wreak havoc if left to his own "selfish" devices. His only moral constraint is that given to him by God and the church. According to this view, man must follow the Ten Commandments handed down to him by God through Moses. If men do not follow God's Commandments, God will punish them on this earth and after death. Men will only do right because of fear of God's wrath.

"Sowell asserts that the vision of contemporary intellectuals (progressives) today is based on an ages old view that sees problems as an outgrowth of social institutions. "In this vision, oppression, poverty, injustice and war are all products of existing institutions—problems whose solutions require changing those institutions, which in turn require changing the ideas behind those institutions."[19] Is Professor Sowell saying that the progressive view is one of hope and that their recommendations are part of some sort of exalted view about actually solving problems? Are we to assume that progressive criticism of institutions such as capitalism and the church are valid? Is he perhaps giving them too much credit? Claiming to have hope for men by forcing them to sacrifice, as the progressives do, is hardly a hopeful concept. Such a hope sounds like a politician's false promise never to come true.

"One must wonder if progressives today really threaten to destroy the most advanced, the most just and affluent civilization in the history of the world out of hope for a better future. There is a problem with cause and effect here.

"Whether you receive your view of man's nature from Hobbes or Hume, you cannot derive the principles of a free society and the anti-principles of a slave society from the same source; from the view that man is imperfect. The logic of ideas in practice is inexorable; you cannot get around it. If the conservatives and the progressives both have the same basic view of man, the result will be the same social solution...and it is not hope but rubble.

---

[19] Ibid Page 76

"Yet, the question regarding man's nature is the foundation upon which all human action must be based. The answer to that question indicates not only how intellectuals think men will act but how governments will treat them. Does man have rights? Is he to be a slave to the needs of others? These questions are important. The only difference between conservatives and progressives is not that progressives see certain institutions as needing change and that conservatives do not; the vital question is "from where does man derive his mandate for moral action?" Political debates and revolutionary change are not about merely changing institutions; they are about understanding man's nature and dealing with him accordingly.

"When Barack Obama says he believes in service to the community, working for and dying for others, the conservatives can only say, 'so do we'. They may counter the progressives with arguments for faith, hope and charity, but the progressives also talk about faith, hope and charity.

"The dilemma for the conservatives on this issue is that they've failed to identify the principles that truly reflect what is wrong with the progressive views. They are on the same side as the progressives because they both advocate altruism as their fundamental principle. They have failed to recognize that man's true nature is not that he is imperfect but that he is a creature of reason, a creature perfectly suited for survival and success. The result: the conservatives have nothing to offer against the views of the progressives who also see man as cognitively incapable of understanding reality.

"To continue with Doctor Sowell, "In the tragic vision, barbarism is always waiting in the wings and civilization is simply "a thin crust over a volcano." (This quote is from Havelock Ellis. The full statement is "All civilization has from time to time become a thin crust over a volcano of revolution.") The metaphor, "a thin crust over a volcano" used to describe the position of civilization against barbarism is illustrious of the problem that conservatives create for themselves. If civilization is truly a thin crust over a volcano, then what is the point of trying to create a better society? Eventually, the volcano will erupt (into revolution) and destroy that thin layer. If this is our choice, then why should we continue living on that thin crust? (Parentheses mine)

"Unfortunately, this is the false alternative that conservatives create for themselves. A "thin crust" versus an inevitable explosion is hardly a choice. When they create such false alternatives based on non-essentials, they end up rationalizing false views and eventually taking the side of the progressives. To place one's enemies, the enemies of freedom, in the position of "a volcano", means you know they will win.

"Is civilization truly "a thin crust over a volcano"? Or are the principles of a proper society based upon something more fundamental (and enduring) in man's nature that must be recognized and accommodated by government; facts and principles that endure and never explode. Shouldn't we instead strive for a vision of man that will acknowledge his value and thereby help in the creation of a bulwark against the explosion of violence and barbarism? I submit that this bulwark is what the Founders of our nation attempted to create, and their vision of man was not at all "tragic". (Parenthesis mine)

""In the tragic vision, social contrivances seek to restrict behavior that leads to unhappiness, even though these restrictions themselves cause a certain amount of unhappiness. It is a vision of trade-offs, rather than solutions, and a vision of wisdom distilled from the experiences of the many rather than the brilliance of a few."[20]

"This means that civilization is nothing more than "social contrivances" designed to restrict immoral living in order to make a trade-off, to create a balance between immorality (selfishness) and self-sacrifice (the good). What is being traded here is your decision to be productive in return for the government getting a piece of your production. Your punishment for committing the crime of surviving is that you have to pay people who cannot survive.

---

[20] Ibid Page 78

Remember, this is the conservative view. And, to prove it, notice that the desire of President Obama (or President Biden) to "re-distribute" wealth is considered by the conservatives to be "the brilliance of a few". (Last parenthesis mine)

"I would like to take issue with the criticism that progressives represent an elite that thinks it is smart enough to make decisions for us. Certainly, they think they are such an elite. But the truth is there is no such elite telling us what to do and how to think. Most of them talk only to themselves. The concept of elitism is a strawman designed to engender hate from the conservative "yokels". Certainly, progressives love when conservatives give them that position of power (and Dr. Sowell certainly does), but the truth is we don't have to listen to them and few of us actually do. Indeed, regardless of what we say about them, they will keep spouting their "superior" knowledge as long as libraries buy their books. That is in the nature of progressivism not elitism.

"And to prove that conservatives have no understanding of their own position, Doctor Sowell says, "The conflict between these two visions goes back for centuries. Those with the tragic vision and those with the vision of the anointed do not simply happen to differ on a range of policy issues. They necessarily differ because they are talking about very different worlds which exist inside their minds. Moreover, they are talking about different creatures who inhabit that world, even though both call these creatures human beings, for the nature of those human beings is also fundamentally different as seen in the two visions."[21]

"I'm sure the conservatives appreciate that criticism.

"Professor Sowell does not seem to recognize that both philosophical skeptics and conservative philosophers such as Hobbes and Burke saw man in essentially the same way. They both saw man as incapable of understanding reality, in other words, as imperfect. How can the same basic view of man lead to two different solutions in politics? (It) can't. Progressivism and conservatism are two contrary (rather than contradictory) ideas based on the same premise that will inevitably lead to the same result: enslavement.

"The reason the conservatives use non-essentials (tragic vision versus anointed vision) in separating conservatives from progressives is that they must evade the hidden motive of the conservative vision. I doubt that Professor Sowell and other conservatives know that their argument on the issue of man's nature is weak, and I doubt that they have an ulterior motive. I think they truly want freedom, but even they cannot escape the logical consequences of their arguments. The truth is that their view of man is a false attack, and it implies government action against him that would control his individual moral

---

[21] Ibid Page 78

choices. The real goal of religious conservatives, since they became politically prominent, has been to make room for faith in a world that is constantly being transformed by the power of reason. Politically, for the conservatives, that goal can only be accomplished by authoritarian theocracy.

"Since religious conservatives want to restrict what they consider to be immoral acts, their advocacy of capitalism necessarily leaves much to be desired. The conflict takes place when you attempt to graft the control of immoral acts (determined by God in the Bible) on a system that is based on the individual's right to decide for himself what is moral action. What the conservative considers to be immoral and selfish may actually be moral and life-serving when viewed from the perspective of the individual and his life (As example, look at past efforts to control sexual activities and attitudes which fall hardest on women and gays).

"Economic conservatives therefore must avoid discussions of morality and stick religiously to economic statistics and the negative consequences of central planning. It also takes some of them to pragmatism, real politick, neo-conservatism and, you guessed it, the inevitability of progressivism (the old "thin crust of the volcano").

"In fact, the conservatives have managed to proclaim the superiority of their own stated enemies. "The two visions differ fundamentally, not only in how they see the world but also in how those who believe in these visions see themselves. If you happen to believe in free markets, judicial restraint, traditional values and other features of the tragic vision, then you are just someone who believes in free markets, judicial restraint and traditional values. There is no personal exaltation resulting from those beliefs. But to be for "social justice" and "saving the environment," or to be "anti-war" is more than just a set of beliefs about empirical facts. This vision puts you on a higher moral plane as someone concerned and compassionate, someone who is for peace in the world, a defender of the downtrodden, and someone who wants to preserve the beauty of nature and save the planet from being polluted by others less caring. In short, one vision makes you somebody special and the other vision does not. These visions are not symmetrical."[22] In short, progressives are good and conservatives are evil.

"Imagine the following conversation: "Why aren't conservatives good?" asks the conservative.

""They favor capitalism and self-interest", say the progressives.

""No, we don't" say the conservatives. "We want capitalism because we believe that is the best way to achieve "the highest good." We're just like you."

""How is that possible? Isn't capitalism about greedy acquisition and theft from the poor?" ask the progressives.

""Yes, it is," say the conservatives. "But we can control that through regulations and Anti-trust. We just want to manipulate the market so it can achieve 'the highest good.'"

""So do we," say the progressives. "That's why we want to re-distribute wealth."

""But that will create distortions in the marketplace. We don't want any distortions, do we?"

""See," say the progressives. "You really don't mean what you say. You are really just working for those greedy capitalists."

"This is called "the moral argument" and it is based on the premise that all human action should be without self-interest; that it should be "for others". The conservatives have no answer except to say they agree; they just want to accomplish social wellbeing in a different way, a way that works. This is not the way to say you stand for the right.

""Trickle down," say the progressives. "Capitalism has failed. We've got a better way. Let's just take the money."

"The problem for the conservatives is that pesky little word "self-interest". Because of their altruistic (utilitarian) premises, they just can't get around the idea that capitalism is really about self-interest. They wish it weren't so.

""But the Founders established our traditions and those are good, aren't they?"

"The progressives just chuckle at the hypocrisy.

"Indeed, self-interest is a pretty bad motivation if you believe that man's duty is to sacrifice for others. The conservatives are stuck with the contradiction. And the dubious utilitarian argument just doesn't seem to work when you've got those left-wing protesters out on the streets in front of television cameras complaining about systemic racism, systemic greed and riches and theft and MONEY, even wild parties and lots of sex too. Once you lay that guilt trip on them, conservatives shut up and vote the way the progressives want.

"The progressives have been successful in manipulating the conservatives into being the agents of "self-interest". Not only have they painted the conservatives into the corner as stealthy advocates of it, but they are also the teachers who have put the proverbial dunce caps on them as well. The conservatives simply cannot get out of that corner until they learn to claim the moral high ground. They are evading the moral arguments for capitalism, the very arguments that hard working Americans would champion and support. These are the arguments that they need if they are to establish the moral fervor necessary to withstand the same progressive arguments that have silenced them for so long - and that make the conservatives into weaklings hardly worth getting out of bed to vote for.

"How do they find that moral high ground? You might be surprised to hear that they can't do it by quoting God at every turn. No voter is going to get excited about "moral contrivances" designed to restrict immoral actions. Voters are only going to get excited about the possibility of working hard and keeping their earnings. They need a "selfish" reason to vote not politicians who are afraid to say "capitalism", "individual rights" and "freedom" and "the pursuit of happiness". They need politicians who are going to make the moral case for individual rights and property rights. They don't want moral cowards.

"Conservatives have to reject the view that man's nature is part of a "tragic" vision. They must stop focusing their arguments on the idea that man is fallible, that he can only survive by sacrificing for others; they must stop implying that men will always make the wrong moral decisions and that government is there to hold him back. These arguments do not justify freedom; they justify coercion against individuals. Under this view, choosing to live, to create values, to trade values, to organize companies, to be productive, to think, to produce, to make a (huge) profit, to flourish and to enjoy life are all immoral decisions. Why do they agree with that vision of man?

"Conservatives must learn to embrace morality by embracing the pursuit of happiness and by being guiltlessly proud of it. It is not a sin to declare that man is a creature with the ability to reason, to choose and to enjoy life.

"As I (have written elsewhere), "Altruism is not the moral base of a capitalist system. We can't have a successful capitalist system if we just want to help people. Capitalism requires an independent mind. We must want men to be free to think, we must know living requires work, we must honor the independent mind and we must give credit where credit is due. Altruism requires a mind ruled by the edicts of superiors and it tells man that to be moral he only needs to follow the easiest path of all: the road of sacrifice as virtue. Capitalism requires integrity. Altruism requires that man fight his bodily nature with his spiritual code. Capitalism requires honesty. Altruism requires that one deceive one's own mind. Capitalism requires justice. Altruism requires that justice be suspended among men, that men do society's work by being unjust towards those who refuse to sacrifice. Capitalism requires productiveness. Altruism requires that the productive give away their money. Capitalism requires pride. Altruism requires both humility in some men and pretentiousness in others. Capitalism requires principled action based on abstract concepts tied to reality. Altruism requires Kantian mush, vague, disconnected equivocations, switching contexts, unintelligibility, one reality that is inaccessible by the mind and a second mental universe that is incompetent. Capitalism is a challenge to the individual and it demands his best effort. Altruism demands only envy and hatred of capitalism."

"The Founders understood that man should be free to make a better life. They knew that he can only do so by identifying reality, understanding what is in his best interest, knowing or discovering how to achieve it and then taking action. They understood that man was good because they, the Founders, had achieved success in life by means of study, practical action and reason. This is the source of our "rugged individualism"; the source of a unique image of a man with the self-confidence and the ability to survive in the wilderness. "Daniel Boone was a man!" This is why they based our society upon the principles of "life, liberty and the pursuit happiness". This is why they limited the power of government to violate those rights.

"The Founders understood that freedom makes possible the unhindered pursuit of values. And in order to produce values, a man must have the ability to identify what values are, what human purposes they achieve and not only how to create them but also how to price them, deliver them and discuss their features and benefits for the purchaser. A value can only be created as an outgrowth of a rational process, a thinking process that identifies what is in the maker's and the buyer's self-interest. Capitalism is not about greed but about individual rights and self-interest. This is not the tragic view.

"A value must fulfill a proudly selfish need for man because its creation depends upon a person's choice, and in order for you to choose a life-enhancing value, it must first be validated by a process of reason that justifies it in terms of benefit to the valuer. There is no other way to think about values.

"Needless to say, conservatives will never argue for capitalism on this basis, and this is why you see Professor Sowell attempting to explain the differences between conservatives and progressives on grounds other than an individual's moral right to the pursuit of his own individual happiness.

"Contrast the politician of today with an architect such as Frank Lloyd Wright and you will see the difference between a valuer and a nihilist. Wright and his designs are pro-man, pro-life, pro-value. The architect expressed his love of life and of values by means of manipulating natural resources to express in his buildings a concept of priceless utility combined with ultimate beauty and the enjoyment of both. The designs of his buildings expressed so much more than just lines and corners; they expressed the beauty of nature, the organization of natural resources and the feelings of comfort and relaxation. The emphasis on values is so implicit yet so real that you must grow intellectually in order to comprehend the beauty within the mind of the architect. He brings you to a new evaluation of man and all that is possible through him. This is what America and American business is all about, this love of values, this moral high ground, not the sleazy smile of a person who has done nothing notable except write grants for non-profit (and unprofitable) organizations, write books about nothing that he has done and become famous for it. Contrast a Wright with an Obama and you'll see the difference between a person who creates values and one who re-distributes them. One is a businessman who creates life as a natural outgrowth of loving life and the other creates poverty through flim flam and manipulation. One inspires the upward glance; the other inspires the glance of hatred and envy aimed at any man with a mind. And conservatives want to call him an elite with hope for the future.

"This refusal by the conservatives to defend capitalism on proper moral grounds has created a situation where there is no opposition to the progressives; and it opens the door to the vilest forms of nihilism. At every turn, President Obama, as President, destroyed values. Whether it was American free enterprise, the sacredness of contract, the rewarding of failure, the bailouts, the dismissing of our allies, the hand (full of cash) extended toward dictators, unilateral nuclear disarmament, socialized medicine, anti-gun policies, Cap and Trade, Union Card Check – everything he did destroyed values.

...

"This "victory of nihilism" that Obama has wrought is clearly the fault of conservatives who did not fight for capitalism and freedom in a way that defended the rights of Americans to live, succeed and enjoy life. It has destroyed our ability to produce abundance, but more importantly, it may have destroyed our futures. And because conservatives have too easily attempted bi-partisan cooperation with progressives for so many decades, Americans will think that the conservatives will continue to do what they've always done – promise smaller government but deliver bigger budgets. They will know that the politicians will continue lying to them.

"In order to defend limited government, we must defend the capitalist system that is its product. In order to defend the good men who are living moral lives by being productive, we must have a different view of man, a view that sees man (not as a tragic joke who needs to be free because he is stupid), but as a healthy, strong, and independent thinker who can make the right decisions about his life and actions – and who needs to be free because it is his right. Only when we defend man's competence, can those who advocate limited government and individual rights capture the moral high ground.

"The Founders did not create a society that was based on the imperfectability of man. If any of them expressed that view, they were wrong. In fact, they created a society based on the Enlightenment view of man as a creature of reason and they established the governmental machinery that protected man's mind from the encroachment of unreason. They wanted to foster free expression, free thought, free choices, free markets, in short, liberty; the right of man to live as he chooses without the imposition of government – including without the imposition of a religion.

"Jefferson said, "Millions of innocent men, women, and children, since the introduction of Christianity, have been burnt, tortured, fined, imprisoned; yet we have not advanced one inch towards uniformity (of religious thought). What has been the effect of coercion? To make one half the world fools, and the other half hypocrites. To support roguery and error all over the earth. Let us reflect that it is inhabited by a thousand millions of people. That these profess probably a thousand different systems of religion. That ours is but one of that thousand. That if there be but one right, and ours that one, we should wish to see the 999 wandering sects gathered into the fold of truth. But against such a majority we cannot effect this by force. Reason and persuasion are the only practicable instruments. To make way for these, free enquiry must be indulged; and how can we wish others to indulge it while we refuse it ourselves."[23] (Parentheses mine)

"Many of the original settlers of our country were concerned about finding a place where they could practice their religion. They were not all concerned about spreading their faith to other men. They had experienced too much of that imposed upon them in Europe. They wanted the freedom to experience and practice their religious principles in their own way. In fact, many of these sects saw religious faith as an individual choice to be contemplated and enjoyed individually in the wondrous and scenic nature that our new land provided. Many of them clearly understood the importance of religious tolerance. We should follow their example.

"I think the insecurity of many religious conservatives stems from a feeling that religion will someday go away. I think they are afraid that they don't have an argument against science and reason and they want to convince us that if religion goes away so will freedom. Many of them probably believe this. Their insistence that reason and science (secularism) will turn man into a wild wanton sinful brute is the flaw in their argument. Their belief that man cannot be good without God is intolerant and insulting to many Americans who have fought for

---

[23] The Notes on Virginia, Thomas Jefferson

religious freedom while also holding to their own philosophies or religions. In truth, only free men want to think the highest thoughts; they want to traverse the frontiers of the planet and the universe. If they discover God at the end, it is their right to think as they wish. If they do not, that is their right as well. In truth, only free men can be perfect and that perfection is not a threat to God. Perhaps it is the road to God.

"I would like to state that I admire Thomas Sowell tremendously. His defense of capitalism through these many years has undoubtedly required heroic courage and intellectual honesty considering our present political climate. He is truly an admirable man who deserves the highest praise. With that said, I think he is wrong on this crucial issue. If you believe that man is tragically imperfect, the logical conclusion is that you should not leave him free; you should restrict his freedom. And this is clearly what Doctor Sowell advocates when he says that "social contrivances seek to restrict behavior that leads to unhappiness, even though these restrictions themselves cause a certain amount of unhappiness."

"In fact, the correct view of man is that he is a creature who should be allowed to discover his moral perfection through his freely chosen thoughts and actions. Because man is perfect in his ability to reason, he must be free. If there is anything in this world to "believe" in, it is the glorious possibilities of man. Only a free man can be moral."

A man under duress can only experience a false sense of morality if his actions comply with the pressure imposed upon him. Absent freedom, the effort to make him comply with rationalistically derived dogma is a form of force. Reality will not comply.[24]

In truth, the election of Donald Trump in 2024 was a victory for capitalism (in a sense). The voters rejected altruism implicit in candidate Harris' invocation of totalism (communism) that is fueled by the arguments for communism. The Trump campaign did not argue for individualism and capitalism. It was the voters who realized the corruption of the left – they did it on their own.

---

[24] The Conservative's Dilemma by Robert Villegas

Pragmatism

For those who think that the second Trump administration may succeed at turning our economy around, we must point out that virtually every major thinker today believes that pragmatism is an effective philosophy that achieves tangible results. As I have shown in my two books on pragmatism, this philosophy is decidedly impractical. By exposing the idea that pragmatism is not based upon practical action, I point out that its foundation is the indeterminacy of Kant and Hume.

How has indeterminacy influenced, not only the human mind, but the actions men take? When Hume declared that there was no such thing as necessity or cause and effect, he was considered to have been doing science. His contention that we could not see the connection between action and consequence was the false premise that led Kant to sever the connection between the mind and reality, which made men assume that there was no source for human understanding.

In my book, *How Pragmatism Destroyed a World*[25], I wrote:

"Kant theorized that the world is separated into two realms: the phenomenal and noumenal. The

---

[25] https://amzn.to/489le6r

phenomenal realm, according to Kant, includes all our experiences and appearances of the world as we know it, whereas the noumenal realm consists of noumena. The noumena, or Kant's controversial 'thing-in-itself', are unknowable entities that exist outside of our experience and are not under the laws of determinism or time."[26]

"The pragmatist tells us, man can only take bold leaps and then examine if they worked. If you want to know why our nation is in so much trouble it is the "problem solvers" who are the problem. For them a "theory" is blind but there is no knowledge anyway. Man is only an automaton without connection to reality.

"The fatal flaw of this philosophy is that it considers knowledge and cause and effect to be superfluous. Only activism, trial and error and "bold action" can make a difference. This is how pragmatists sell themselves on the idea that they are "results-oriented" as we will see. They don't realize that their premises are self-refuting; they have yet to figure out that they are not able to ascertain results according to their own "theories".

"You may still think there is nothing wrong with being results-oriented. Let me point out that without

26   https://www.123helpme.com/essay/Immanuel-Kant-And-The-Phenomenal-And-Noumena-436008

knowledge, without standards, without a view of what truth is and how it is achieved, a pragmatist cannot *be* results-oriented because his standard for evaluating results will always be flawed. He can only be left with results that "feel" right based upon subconscious thoughts or the results of polls among the people.

"Individuals and their rights are always swept up into the spider web of the pragmatist technocrat who only has thoughts of collective power and democracy rolling around in his head. He is a person who thinks he is smart enough to decide for others what is in their interests, but he brings to his "intelligence" the most mundane of thoughts, disconnected and without form.

"How can the technocrat solve problems when he has no standard for deciding what is correct knowledge that leads to correct action? It is simple, the pragmatist only has one appeal left and it is an appeal that comes automatically, from his gut, so to speak.

"When someone proposes an action or project, he looks to his gut. If he thinks the people in his life might dislike him for the idea, he will immediately bury it and find out what the majority wants. So, what feels "best" to a pragmatist is what makes him feel safe and taken care of, and what makes him feel best of all is the approval of others. So, if he wants others to approve his proposals, he must tailor his proposals toward making people happier and this means altruism and collectivism, love of others and the desire to please them. That is what the pragmatist uses as his "logical" test: what will make others happy.

"So, what moves a pragmatist? What people say, what they think and especially what they feel strongly about. So, when something happens in society that gets people angry, starts riots and violence – well disapproval from the rioters causes the pragmatist's gut to churn and the only thing he can do is appease the crowd. They must be right because they are angry.

"So, pragmatists almost automatically find themselves advancing altruism and collectivism because those ideas make them feel good, regardless of the consequences. Don't be surprised at the "heroic" efforts by pragmatists in high positions to include accommodation of the evilest people on the planet. They ignore principles, knowledge and truth for the sake of ameliorating their gut feelings – that is their motivation and nothing more.

"The question before us now is how the wrong philosophy can bring about global catastrophe. As we know, according to our leaders, dealing with the pandemic required a national shutdown of the economy ordered by the Federal government, specifically by the Trump administration. Is this what we needed for survival, an order to stay in our homes and hide? The obvious question was, "How can man use his mind to survive if he is given an order to hunker down in his home?" The answer should have been not to hunker down but to attack the problem with direct action. As I will show, this is not what happened.

"As we saw, the immediate consequence of this order was the passage of legislation to send checks to millions of Americans to help them weather the economic shutdown. What is the philosophy that brought this solution about? How is it that men thought the best way to deal with the shutdown was to spend money we didn't have? The cause of this insanity is the philosophy of pragmatism which dominates the universities our leaders attended.

"So, what did the pragmatists teach in the universities? We will let another pragmatist tell us.

""Let the will of the state act, then, instead of that of the individual. Let an institution be created which shall have for its object to keep correct doctrines before the attention of the people, to reiterate them perpetually, and to teach them to the young; having at the same time power to prevent contrary doctrines from being taught, advocated, or expressed. Let all possible causes of a change of mind be removed from men's apprehensions. Let them be kept ignorant, lest they should learn of some reason to think otherwise than they do. Let their passions be enlisted so that they may regard private and unusual opinions with hatred and horror."[27]

Marxist/pragmatist ideas, such as anti-capitalism are based fundamentally upon the indeterminacy and value hatred of Hume, Kant and Dewey. The dangers of indeterminacy and nihilism are found in the derivative premises that proceed from them, the divisions, the anti-capitalism, the altruism (sacrifice), dis- and mis-information, and the anti-individualism found in ideas such as class struggle, critical theory, critical race theory, DEI, ESG, and anti-male hatred that all lead to confusion and weakness within the minds of men. Such anti-concepts prepare the human mind (that they create) for the acceptance of totalitarianism (a society of total control of the individual).

These ideas of indeterminacy lead, eventually, to the pragmatist idea that reality is mere perception, that collective consciousness creates reality, that there is

---

[27] *The Fixation of Belief, Charles Sanders Peirce* (one of the fathers of pragmatism and also a father of modern education)

no cause and effect, that the end justifies the means, and short-term results define human efficacy until they stop working.

Additionally, in this book, *"How Pragmatism Destroyed a World"*, chapter **Pragmatism and America**, I wrote:

"The American pragmatists among our leaders (including Republicans and Democrats, but especially the Business Roundtable[28]) think that Peirce and Dewey gave them the means for making a better world. They confidently believe that pragmatism is like a magic formula; "practice these methods and the future will be better". They consider themselves doers, men of action, men of practical results. Yet, they acknowledge that knowledge is impossible and that it is practical to use trial and error to see how things work out. This is because they have no practical philosophical foundation. The rest they pull out of the prevailing cultural premises. They are like the ancient Greeks, still trying to figure out the one in the many with the only difference being that the Greeks were actually focused on reality (air, fire, water and earth) while today's pragmatists have no

---

[28] The Business Roundtable (purportedly) is an association of chief executive officers of America's leading companies working to promote a thriving U.S. economy and expanded opportunity for all Americans (supposedly) through sound public policy. (parentheses mine) In fact, the Business Roundtable is a lobbying group that collectively advances leftist policies in order to appease governmental progressive (altruist and collectivist) policies.

such foundation. They are stuck in a cosmology of doubt and fear over man's role in the world and they proclaim that they know how to get things done. The Greeks developed logic and reason while the pragmatists of today reject those concepts.

"Pragmatism starts with the Kantian and Humean premises that man is essentially incapable of knowing reality. This premise leads pragmatists to avoid studying reality; they never care about science and facts and truth; they only care about the opinions of "the people". Pseudo-science is their stock in trade. They start from the premise that a proper focus on reality should be on problems as they come up with little regard for how those problems developed in the first place. They assume that "the problem is here" and the only important thing is how we deal with it.

"How did Kant lay the foundation for pragmatism? He did it by blocking the human mind from reality, giving man no choice but to assume that there was no way available for human understanding."

"So, for Kant and his followers, the phenomena are mere "appearances" while the noumena are inaccessible to the human mind. On such a foundation, the only conclusion men can draw is that action can only be blind because morality is blind, knowledge is blind, and certainty is impossible. If the only thing you can "know" is appearance, then what can you know? How can you know? And, most importantly, how then can you act?

"Kant and Hume came from the tradition known as skepticism which holds that "no objective or certain knowledge of anything by anyone is possible. In other words, that whatever we call knowledge is really a guess, a hunch, a subjective feeling, a probability or whatever you wish to call it, but not true knowledge."[29]

"This is the mindset of virtually every politician and certainly of Donald Trump who is also a product of the American University (Wharton). People with uncertain knowledge then have no recourse but to identify what has worked in the past and hope it is still working. If you consider that an intelligent approach, I question your understanding of intelligence. So, who did they turn to? The Chinese.

"But wait, didn't this pandemic start in China? What does that have to do with pragmatism? It is hard to call the Chinese communists pragmatists because of their Marxist bent but, in fact, Mao was an avid reader of Hume and other European philosophers. You might say they "expanded his mind" and made him into a man focused on practical results such as

---

[29] Founders of Western Philosophy – Thales to Hume lecture by Dr. Leonard Peikoff

the result of getting rid of Chinese property owners so he could live in their palatial homes. Judging reality by means of his success at political and monetary gain was his claim to fame. He was a pragmatist; he acted first and then thought later, if he thought at all.

"The Chinese communists are pragmatists par excellence. Even many American corporate executives admire their "practical results" in the age of party-style fascism. This is not the first time American leaders have admired fascists."[30]

In fact, pragmatism, the philosophy of indeterminism, holds that to be a pragmatist makes you practical. Yet, every tenet of Marxism is impractical. Economically, Marxists hold that re-distribution and economic regulations are real politik, that they work. In fact, both re-distribution and economic regulations distort the law of supply and demand and devastate the world's economies. On the other hand, they hold that altruism, self-sacrifice, is a practical morality. They promise that when men sacrifice on the pyre of altruism, the productive are devastated morally and forced to live unproductively. Finally, their ideas that the end justifies the means, that perception is reality, that

---

[30] How Pragmatism Destroyed a World by Robert Villegas Hardcover https://amzn.to/3WXt66q

motivating people through their emotions, catharsis, is a practical way to get citizens to do what the elites want them to do, that anti-intellectuality is the best mental state for the average man, and that men should be slaves.

Indeed, the ignorance of the left is staggering. Their anti-capitalism, altruism, reliance on catharsis and indeterminacy (that is a form of anti-reason) are the causes of their failures, and the means for their demise.

Finally, the idea of real politik, that political actions must be harsh, cruel, hateful, and especially cynical about man, that people are stupid and deserving of the force that government can wield over them. For instance,

"…when you put a campaign together and you hire young people to do work, let me tell you exactly what you tell these people, what I would tell them, "Not only am I not interested in your f…king opinion, I'm not even going to call you by your name. You are 23 years old. I really don't give a sh.t what you think. And let me tell you another error, a huge f…king, is when people said, 'campaigns need to reflect progressive values'; no they don't, no they don't, campaigns are authoritarian by their nature. If I were running a 2028 campaign, and I had some little snot-nosed 23 year old saying, 'I'm going to resign if you don't do this', not only would I fire that little mother f...ker on the spot, I'd find out who hired him and fire that person on the spot. I'm really not interested in your funny farm stupid, jackass opinion..."[31]

The idea that politics is a cynical pursuit of power exposes the utter impracticality of the philosophy of pragmatism. It is, in effect, a compartmentalization of human thinking that argues for the practicality of destroying human values. The key goal and purpose of pragmatism is to make people doubt their own minds.

How does one define a moral code and then live by it? One method is to look around at other codes, analyze them, and then decide which code to live by. Another method is to start from scratch, define a moral premise and then build appropriate actions from this starting point.

Indeed, moral codes don't exist in a vacuum. They do not hang in mid-air to be plucked and then digested. Each code stands on a foundation that gives rise to it, basic observations about the nature of reality and its meaning for the life of man. These are metaphysical and epistemological in nature and are implicit within the code of actions possible to man. For instance, if you believe that knowledge is gained by revelation

---

[31] James Carville

from God and that the universe is hostile to man, you will develop a moral code that requires ritualized propitiation of God through self-sacrifice.

On the other hand, if one holds that knowledge is gained by reason and the universe is benevolent to man, your moral code will free you to pursue values defined by your mind. You are freed from the requirement to propitiate and sacrifice to any other entity. You are free to learn about nature and create your well-being in a world open to happiness and self-fulfillment. And, most importantly, you are able to self-correct and make things better.

The difference between the two approaches above is that between the willing slave and the explorer. The universe is not divided by the "devil" and God but by mindlessness versus knowledge, the world of the irrational versus the world of the rational.

A view of morality, such as that found in altruism, uses man's capacity for pleasure and the fact that he is alive, has a mind, that he wants to live and to think, is used by altruists as proof of man's evil, turns every man into his own enemy, his own accuser, and his own self-hater. Such is the evil of the idea that man must sacrifice his mind and values for the sakes of others.

If the universe, the realm of reality, is evil, what is the sense of sacrificing to a non-existent good? What could the act of sacrificing possibly mean? What is the purpose of living in turmoil over the nature of existence when there is no existence, no necessity? This means that altruism is a self-contradiction, a worthless act of dying.

The truth, of course, is that there is no good or evil in the inanimate universe. Value is a matter of human judgment of the relationship between inanimate objects and the mind of man. Each man is a unique creature who needs pleasure and reason both of which lead to a proper moral code that liberates man to act for his own benefit.

Book Shelf

If you want to understand these issues more thoroughly, I suggest you read the following books from my bookshelf:

Man in Denial by Robert Villegas
https://amzn.to/3VfPur3

Individualism by Robert Villegas
https://amzn.to/3NbstRx

The History of Altruism by Robert Villegas
https://amzn.to/4dyI0pj

Crushing the Alinsky Radicals by Robert Villegas
https://amzn.to/3YaVOSj

Nihilism: and its Role in the World by Robert Villegas
https://amzn.to/4eHk6sW

The REAL Purpose Driven Life by Robert Villegas
https://amzn.to/48d75F1

Alcoholism and Addiction - A Secular Ten-Step Program by Robert Villegas
https://amzn.to/3AdJW8V

Left versus Right – A False Choice by Rober Villegas
https://amzn.to/3U8QX1I

EGOnomics – Finding your Full Ego by Robert Villegas
https://amzn.to/3BLCouJ

How Pragmatism Destroyed a World by Robert Villegas
https://amzn.to/489le6r

Pragmatism on Display by Robert Villegas by Robert Villegas
https://amzn.to/3UbPZSc

Understanding the Modern Mind by Robert Villegas
https://amzn.to/4h8vCze

Ayn Rand's Moral Code by Robert Villegas
https://amzn.to/4dPrXn1

The New Totalitarianism – Quo Vadis? By Robert Villegas
https://amzn.to/3BGAbR1

The Logical Fallacy of Altruism by Robert Villegas
https://amzn.to/404aR1H

The Scourge of Racism and the Cure by Robert Villegas
https://amzn.to/3YtT9U9

What Harvard and Princeton Don't Want You to Know by Robert Villegas https://amzn.to/4evb5Ta

Capitalism Doesn't Fail by Robert Villegas
https://amzn.to/3ZuiGwJ

Selling Short on America – George Soros by Robert George
https://amzn.to/4fQu3oG

Atlas Shrugged by Ayn Rand
https://amzn.to/4eXq3Bw

Anthem by Ayn Rand
https://amzn.to/3ZtSF0G

Capitalism: The Unknown Ideal by Ayn Rand
https://amzn.to/3BaYfM1

For the New Intellectual – the Philosophy of Ayn Rand
https://amzn.to/4igYUfO

Economics in One Lesson by Henry Hazlitt
https://amzn.to/3OBe3ei

Human Action by Ludwig von Mises
https://amzn.to/49esPAU

Socialism by Ludwig von Mises
https://amzn.to/4ihmpVK

Behind the Ritual Mask by Robert Villegas
https://amzn.to/4gfjQSi

Ayn Rand's Normative Ethics – The Virtuous Egoist
by Dr. Tara Smith
https://amzn.to/49iXA7T

Contact the Author
Robertv1989@outlook.com

Robert Villegas is an American writer born in Weslaco, TX. He is an independent philosopher with a strong focus on the practical consequences of ideas. He considers the philosophy of ideas to be a central factor in creating a better society and he offers both a critical discussion of modern philosophy as well as practical solutions and fundamental principles to solve problems associated with pragmatism and indeterminacy. His work stands on its own.

Mr. Villegas spent over twenty-seven years as a UPS executive in Indiana and worked in locations all over Europe such as Germany, England, and Spain. At UPS he worked as a Call Center Manager and Telecommunications Manager. He was involved in helping to transition UPS from paper-based processes to computerized networks and digital record keeping. He worked with early digital technologies and was one of the first telecommunications managers to develop a system for communicating to drivers while they were on their routes.

After leaving UPS, Mr. Villegas started his own sport marketing company specializing in writing sponsorship proposals for race car drivers and other athletes. Clients included Johnny Parsons,

Jeff Ward, Larry Foyt and Alexander Rossi to name a few. He also worked as a technical writer in the burgeoning telecommunications industry in South Florida where he created many successful sales presentations and marketing documents. He also built his company's first website and worked for companies throughout the country including New York City, Boston, San Francisco, Sacramento, Chicago, Miami, Minneapolis, Vancouver BC, and other locations.

In 2015, he began to pursue his life-long goal of becoming a published author and has written about 109 books to date in areas such as novels, theater, religion, poetry, philosophy, and business. During this period, he also wrote over 260 Business Plans mostly for companies in Canada. He also wrote grant proposals and developed grant proposal narratives for several organizations, earning millions of dollars for fire departments and charitable organizations.

He has also served in the US Military as a communications specialist and served his tour of duty during the Vietnam era in Korea near the DMZ. He was raised in Indiana and presently lives in Arizona.

He was educated in Indiana and earned a Degree through the University of the State of NY (Albany) via an external degree program when he came out of the military. He is divorced with three grown children and three grandchildren. Famous relatives include Mexican anti-hero Dimas DeLeon and guitarist and music producer Johnny Garcia of Weslaco, TX

They notice him,
And try to hold him down,
Use all their tricks
To make him be like them.
But when they see
He's breaking ground
They move aside
And let him abide.

The wind touches him.
He knows life is around.
He has resolved
That he will be for real.
And when he speaks,
He loves the sound
Of life inside,
He will abide.

He looks at things
And knows that truth is found
In his insight.
And he bids the world, see.
He knows in ears
His words will drown.
They have decried
He will abide.

For this he knows:
Adventure makes hearts pound.

And for him,
The search for truth
Through every day
Makes his resound.
With all his pride,
He will abide.

Notes

Notes

Notes

Aphrodite

Johnny is a Spanish guitar player with a mysterious past. At a party, he meets the beautiful songstress Aphrodite who is enthralled with his flamenco guitar skills. Later, she learns they have a connection, a particular song they both appear to know. Aphrodite discovers the connection, and through dreams, the two fall in love. The question is whether they will ever be together. https://amzn.to/3xIlmXZ $3.99 Kindle $5.95 softcover

The Odyssey of Amerigo the Founder

Amerigo was born in a time of desperation and dystopia. He was the only man with the vision of a great future. Many repaired to his cause while others swore to destroy him. They wanted his life, his mind and everything he loved. He swore that no matter what they did, he would win the struggle for freedom and a new future.
https://amzn.to/2Qz8h2t $3.99 Kindle $8.95 softcover

Bob and Bobbie

1967 - a town outside Camp Casey, Korea - two young people have come together to challenge a world that makes love impossible.
https://amzn.to/3sZWSpf $2.99 Kindle $5.95 softcover

The Raven Haired Girl

Bobby met Angie 52 years ago in a poor neighborhood in Indianapolis. It was love at first sight. For a few short months, their relationship blossomed into love. They were in love but didn't know how to be in love because they were only fourteen years old.
https://amzn.to/3306plF $2.99 Kindle $6.95 paperback.

Poetic Prose and Poetry

These expressions represent some of Mr. Villegas' deepest thoughts as he lived and traveled throughout the world in locations such as Germany (East and West), Austria, Britain, Spain, Canada, France, Luxembourg, Belgium, the Netherlands, Korea, New York, Miami, San Francisco and other locations. https://amzn.to/3vu7X3B $2.99 Kindle $6.95 softcover

The Lost Poems

These poems were discovered among Mr. Villegas's archives in 2016. Many of them have been read by only Mr. Villegas. Most of these poems were rejected as "not that good". After seeing them again, he has changed his mind. These poems expressive, fresh and spontaneously honest. https://amzn.to/3aPg5nB $3.99 Kindle $6.95 softcover

Adam Reborn – A Short Play

Adam Reborn is a play of symbols. Adam and Eve, as I have portrayed them, are young and heroic people learning to deal with a Paradise and God that are hostile to them. There is no chance of life for them. https://amzn.to/3u9Nr8b $2.99 Kindle $6.95 softcover

The Boy Who Stood Alone

Jonny Payne has just discovered Ayn Rand and his parents don't know what to do. They take him to a priest and a psychologist but his only question is "What is the price of independence? https://amzn.to/3nCG6ve $3.99 Kindle $6.95 paperback.

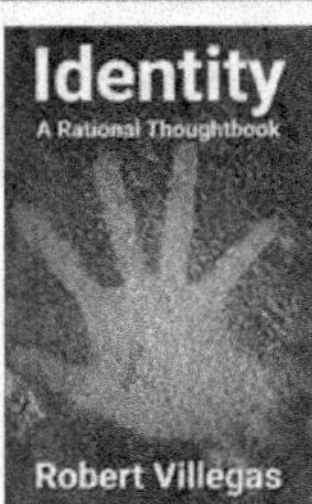

Existence a Rational Thoughtbook

A Rational Thoughtbook is designed for thinking as opposed to reading. It combines brief prescient content with stunning imagery. Existence focuses on the nature of existence and gives you intelligent thoughts to integrate into your life.
https://amzn.to/2RZpsKV $4.99 Kindle $12.95 softcover

Identity

One of the most important goals for any person is to establish intellectual independence. Intellectual independence is the road to "life" independence, which is the ability to earn your own way without help from others. https://amzn.to/3nf9aJn $3.99 Kindle $9.95 softcover

Existence a Rational Thoughtbook

A Rational Thoughtbook is designed for thinking as opposed to reading. It combines brief prescient content with stunning imagery. Existence focuses on the nature of existence and gives you intelligent thoughts to integrate into your life. https://amzn.to/2RZpsKV $4.99 Kindle $12.95 softcover

The Virtue of Independence

One of the most important goals for any person is to establish intellectual independence. Intellectual independence is the road to "life" independence, which is the ability to earn your own way without help from others. https://amzn.to/3awuCV2 $2.99 Kindle $6.95 softcover

Rational Meditation

Rational Meditation is self-meditation. It is thinking about yourself without guilt and without the tenets of modern philosophy (that the world is unknowable, that man is a phony, that ethics and living are only about others). https://amzn.to/3gus9OE $6.99 Kindle $12.95 softcover

History of My Mind

This booklet is the companion to my book entitled Rational Meditation. It utilizes the various exercises of the original book that involve contemplation or meditation and provide space for written input by the reader. https://amzn.to/3gy3hpl $4.69 Kindle $11.95 softcover.

Revelation

These three books are based upon a new perspective on the document named Revelation. Based upon a new theory of the story of Jesus as an invention of the Roman Imperial Cult, these books add significant new evidence for this theory.

Coded Messages in the Pastorals

The first book in the series on Revelation. I see Christianity, as we know it today, as an outgrowth of mostly one mind and one perspective and that is the mind and perspective of Paul the apostle who was the alter-ego for another man who lived and wrote in the AD 80s and AD 90s. https://amzn.to/3xx2Gdm $4.69 Kindle $10.95 softcover

The Seven Letters of Revelation

The second book on the three-book series on Revelation. The idea that Domitian was the author, through John, of Revelation is a relatively new idea. But, if this is true, it answers many questions about the purpose of Revelation and what events led up to it. By connecting the document to Domitian, we are also able to connect it to Pauline Christianity and understand the context for both Christian writings and Revelation. https://amzn.to/3aLekb4 $3.99 Kindle $6.95 softcover

Understanding the Book of Revelation

The third in the three-book series on Revelation, Understanding the Book of Revelation is the third and final book in the series about the conflict between Paul and Domitian over Paul's version of Christianity which is found in the gospels. https://amzn.to/3tWn6dH $5.19 Kindle $8.95 softcover

The Real Purpose-Driven Life
After centuries of being told that it is not about you, it is time to set the record straight. You are a unique individual and your goal in life should be to achieve your own happiness. This book is about helping you accomplish your goals and fixing your purpose firmly in place. It covers not only why you should pursue your goals but how to do it.
https://amzn.to/3ebkhjr $3.99 Kindle $6.95 softcover

The Values and Purpose Workbook
Rather than give you tasks that involve doing a lot of things for other people, I'm am going to tell you that focusing on yourself will reveal your life's purpose and express your passions and freedom. I'm going to start with you.
https://amzn.to/3eQf4wG $2.99 Kindle $6.95 softcover

This Book is About You
Some people move briskly bent on a purpose, concerned only about what they are about. Some people walk by them; and do not even notice. They just keep to their path. This book is about you. It's about time. https://amzn.to/3vFMzss
$2.99 Kindle $5.95 softcover

The REAL Purpose-Driven Life
After centuries of being told that it is not about you, it is time to set the record straight. You are a unique individual and your goal in life should be to achieve your own happiness.
https://amzn.to/2XyrpPf $3.50 Kindle $7.95 softcover

Values and Purpose Workbook
This book is about you. It's about time. After centuries of being told that nothing is about you, it is time to set the record straight. You are a unique individual and your goal in life should be to achieve your happiness. https://amzn.to/2XwlkTv $3.99 Kindle $8.95 softcover

Unkilling Jesus

Who was Paul and what was his role in the creation of Christianity? What was his provenance, and did he meet the resurrected Christ? Who wrote Revelation and what was the document's purpose? Why was Domitian assassinated?

http://amzn.to/2itMCo0 $3.99 Kindle $15.95 softcover

Domitian: The Final Messiah

The central goal of this book is to define the specific themes and concepts that make up Domitian's contribution to Christianity – in a sense, we are defining the specific Domitian overlay to the Christian materials originally developed for Titus.

http://amzn.to/2yWMSlx $2.99 Kindle $6.95 softcover

Paul's Agon and the Mystification of History

Paul and Jesus are joined in one important way; the way of a miracle. They met on the road to Damascus while Paul supposedly pursued Christians. Jesus, in a sense, told Paul to get with the program and stop persecuting his people. In this incident, the Bible tells us that Jesus is already dead, and resurrected. This book argues otherwise.

http://amzn.to/2zSDsuP $5.99 Kindle $19.95 softcover

Christianity on the Arch of Titus

This book explores the "persons" visible on the Triumphant Arch of Titus which is located in the heart of Rome. These people were significant in that they played a role, not only in Rome's conquest of Judaea but also in the creation of Christianity. This book explores those individuals and the roles they played in the creation of one of the most important religious movements in world history.

https://amzn.to/3xz3OgM $3.69 Kindle 10.95 paperback.

The Mark of Titus

Excerpts from the book Unkilling Jesus which highlight some of the key discoveries implied by new theories about the origin of the Jesus Myth. The idea that the Romans invented Christianity is the basic premise of new theories about the origin of Christianity .http://amzn.to/2itMCo0 $3.49 Kindle $5.95 softcover

Contra Religion

This book is designed as a "shorter" explanation of the ideas presented in my larger book, "Behind the Ritual Mask" which seeks to define fundamental principles of religion. I'm hoping this book will serve as a primer for the original book and spur an interest in reading it. http://amzn.to/2yWMSlx $3.99 Kindle $6.95 softcover

Is this the Face that Launched a Thousand Ships?

It was love at first sight. I saw her one day while watching a television program about King Tut, whose tomb had been discovered by Howard Carter years before. I was looking at the famous bust of a beautiful Egyptian Queen. https://amzn.to/3t487x3 $3.99 Kindle $7.95 softcover

The History of Altruism

The History of Altruism is a historical treatment of the development of altruism throughout time from the Paleolithic period to today. It tracks the development of self-sacrifice of primitive man to the advent of altruism as a development from Kant's "duty". It covers a broad sweep of concepts and shows how they influenced modern man, religion and societies through the ages. https://amzn.to/3gN8zgy $4.19 Kindle 14.95 paperback.

These four books by Robert Villegas comprise some of the business books that he has written. As an executive working for several companies, he was able to develop these methods that will help anyone seeking to excel in the business world. These books are:

How to Be a Great Employee – and a Greater Manager

You cannot be a great manager without first being a great employee. And this is something that requires learning, experience and attitude. The attitude comes from you but the learning and experience you should acquire through diligent study and practice. http://amzn.to/2BqdG2i $3.99 Kindle $8.95 softcover

SWOT Analysis Supercharged

A SWOT Analysis is an objective look at the internal and external elements of your organization that impact your success or lack thereof. If done diligently, you will always have a handle on what you need to do to improve season after season.
http://amzn.to/2BCAWYx $3.99 Kindle $6.95 softcover

The Five-Module Call Center Training System

The Five-Module Call Center Training System is designed to assist the Call Center Team Leader in helping his employees quickly upgrade their skills to an acceptable level. http://amzn.to/2B3Svj1 $3.99 Kindle $5.95 softcover

Website Development Methodology

Effective strategic marketing requires the ability to differentiate the website development organization and its deliverables from those of the competition. http://amzn.to/2DnYMqh $2.99 Kindle $12.95 softcover.

These four books comprise a system that can be used by both patients and counselors who are battling Alcoholism and Addiction. Based upon Mr. Villegas's own system developed during his struggle against alcoholism, this system includes:

Alcoholism and Addiction – A Secular Ten-Step Program

This groundbreaking book offers a secular approach to alcoholism unlike that offered by Alcoholics Anonymous. We recommend that every individual going for alcohol and drug-abuse counseling be given a copy of this book which contains the workbook and the two versions of The World's first drunk. http://amzn.to/2md6R9w $3.45 Kindle $11.95 softcover

The Secular Ten-Step Program Workbook

This booklet covers the program developed by Mr. Villegas. It is designed as a workbook with blank spaces for the patient to write his own thoughts as he takes each of the ten steps. Order one copy for each patient in counseling. http://amzn.to/2IrHimS $4.49 Kindle $6.95 softcover

The World's First Drunk – With Counselor Talking Points

This booklet is designed for the counselor as he works with patients during individual or group therapy. It contains helpful tips on discussing the life story of the man who invented alcohol. Order one copy for each patient in counseling. http://amzn.to/2I446Wr $2.99 Kindle $5.95 softcover

The World's First Drunk – Patient Version

This version of the short story contains empty spaces where the patient can answer questions about the life story of the man who invented alcohol. Order one copy for each counselor. http://amzn.to/2IdxBGb $2.99 Kindle $5.95 softcover.

Finding Sponsors Forms Book

This "Forms Book" is intended to provide samples of the forms mentioned in my book "Finding Sponsors for Sport and Entertainment". This will make it possible for you to reproduce these forms in other formats as well as download the forms document from the SponsorProAZ website for use with Microsoft Word. https://amzn.to/3b95yDW $2.99 Kindle $5.50 softcover

Submitting Your Sponsorship Proposal Online

This booklet enables sport teams and concert promoters to submit their sponsorship proposals to companies that accept only online submission of proposals. https://amzn.to/3euzdti $2.99 Kindle $5.95 softcover

The Art of Sponsorship

This short book is based upon Mr. Villegas' book "Finding Sponsors for Sport and Entertainment". It is also based upon a course that he taught for an organization managing Indiana Parks and Recreation facilities. It is, in a sense, a condensation of information from the book geared toward organizations that would like to earn revenues on their facilities through corporate sponsorship. https://amzn.to/3beuVnC $2.99 Kinde $6.95 softcover.

Restarting Your Business After the Pandemic

This new book is designed to help you restart your business after the Coronavirus pandemic. You will find here all the right questions, how you can find the answers and the forms you need to walk through your restart and coming success. https://amzn.to/2QVBNiM $5.15 Kindle $5.95 softcover

Finding Sponsors 1 and 2

This book is written for anyone seeking sponsorship relationships in the sport and entertainment fields. The ideas and principles presented here are applicable to any company, sport team, entertainment company, marketing agency and charitable organization that uses corporate sponsorships to support its activities. Volume 1: https://amzn.to/3ejm1Hp $5.19 Kindle $12.95 softcover Volume 2: https://amzn.to/3eVDoOe $4.69 Kindle $10.95 softcover

How to Write a Sponsorship Proposal

This booklet provide you with some basic guidelines on what to communicate in order to produce a winning sponsorship proposal. These guidelines will focus on what you should be presenting to your potential sponsor to make the best business case for involvement with your team or entertainment company. https://amzn.to/3tpHRxs $2.99 Kindle $6.95 softcover

Hospitality Event Planning Handbook

One key part of your sponsorship activation strategy might be customer hospitality events in conjunction with sporting events. How do you pull off a Hospitality Event for your biggest customers? You may not know how to start, what to do and how to ensure the event is a success. This book can help. http://amzn.to/2mxzpgy $7.95 softcover.

Selling Sponsorship in the Age of the Coronavirus

This book provides suggestions on how sport teams, athletes and concert promoters can mitigate the damage done to their businesses by the economic lockdowns (due to the Coronavirus). It integrates checklists, SWOT Analysis and other valuable business aids into one toolkit that will help you keep your sport and/or genre alive in these difficult times. https://amzn.to/2QVBNiM $5.15 Kindle $5.95 softcover

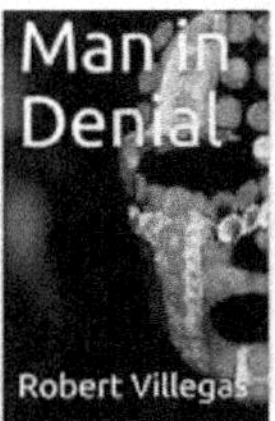

Naming Names in the NT

If psychology has no solid epistemology and metaphysics, how can it stand on its own? I do not think it can and this explains why psychology is in such a sad state today. Yet, before we can put psychology on a solid foundation, philosophy too must advance above the level of puberty. With its base in modern philosophy, even philosophy cannot stand on its own which exposes the real problems with modern psychology. https://amzn.to/3oVTDAQ $5.99 Kindle $9.95 softcover $18.95 hardcover

Finding Your Soft Cry

The purpose of this book is to delve into critical issues about how the human mind has come to the modern position of doubt and despair. The culprits in this matter include the irrationality of both rationalism and skepticism, and, in particular, the child of skepticism known as pragmatism. https://amzn.to/3mRLZF9 $6.99 Kindle $9.60 softcover $26.95 hardcover

The New Totalitarianism – Quo Vadis?

One of the fathers of critical theory was Herbert Marcuse who escaped European dictatorship only by coming to America. America gave him the freedom and protection he needed to destroy capitalism in America. https://amzn.to/2YW9LaS $4.99 Kinde $8.95 softcover.

A Call to Reason

A logical fallacy is a faulty thought process that violates a rule of proper thinking. Correct arguments are defined as proper generalized expressions that define logical truths or knowledge. In effect, a rule of logical reasoning addresses all of the common modes of valid argument while the faulty argument contradicts them. This book examines altruism as a logical fallacy. https://amzn.to/3vdFiB0 $5.99 Kindle $9.95 softcover $18.95 Hardcover

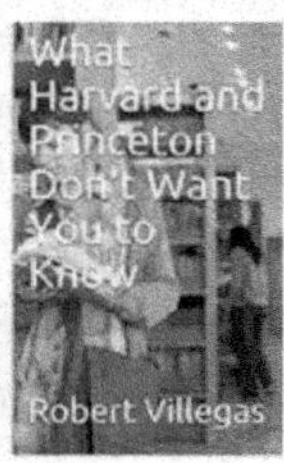

Dachau and Berlin in 1990

This booklet chronicles Mr. Villegas' thoughts during visits to Dachau and Berlin during 1990, disclosing my observations of milestones in German history, past and present, and relating those events to world happenings as they were unfolding at the time. I traveled throughout Germany for much of 1990 while on business. https://amzn.to/3ex578d $2.99 Kindle $6.95 softcover

What Harvard and Princeton Don't Want You to Know

The professors at Harvard and Princeton don't want you to know about the worst ideas in history. This is because they have been pawning these ideas off as true and profound. They have been using them to deceive and manipulate us for centuries. https://amzn.to/3farP5p $5.19 Kindle $9.95 softcover

Defending American Values

This book is made up of several chapters about American values and how they can be defended without a descent into the abyss of dictatorship. The book argues for individual rights and provides reasons why we should fight for them. https://amzn.to/3uMFq9L $3.99 Kinde $5.95 softcover.

Capitalism Doesn't Fail

How many times have we heard the old saw: "Capitalism has failed again" over the course of contemporary events? We heard it during the Great Depression of 1929 after Hoover had invoked tariffs and precipitated economic retaliation and a banking crisis. Along with this question usually came a statement to the effect, that "We can fix capitalism and make it even stronger by issuing economic controls or spending money to stimulate economic activity." https://amzn.to/3xZlAJ6 $4.19 Kindle $10.95 softcover

A Boomer takes on the Far Left

I just learned something about myself – and it isn't very good. In fact, it is very bad. I learned that the opinions of Boomers don't matter any more. We are obsolete in this new age of new knowledge. Anything we think is unimportant and false. I don't think so. https://amzn.to/3tzNqtc $5.19 Kindle $10.95 softcover

Crushing the Alinsky Radicals

The worst enemy of individual rights today is a group of people I call the Alinsky Radicals. These people are now in charge of our culture and temporarily, in charge of government. They are associated, philosophically and politically, with the communists and fascists of the past. They are not your father's liberals. They are the direct descendants of dictators such as Stalin and Mao. In this book, I hope to convince you of the evil of the Alinsky Radicals and to provide the intellectual ammunition you need to eradicate them from society. https://amzn.to/3hbh9WN $3.49 Kindle $8.95 softcover

The Conservative's Dilemma

I wrote this book to ask some important questions about the conservative philosophy of altruism. https://amzn.to/3bfDQ8e $2.99 Kinde $6.95 softcover.

The Biggest Mistakes in History – 2008 to 2016

To be the Chief Executive of the greatest country in the world requires a leader with a great deal of knowledge, experience and reasoning ability. It requires having the very best minds as advisors, minds that the President can count on to give reasoned arguments and detailed knowledge about the important issues of the day. I think it takes a special ability to understand the principle of cause and effect concerning how government action impacts the lives of real people. https://amzn.to/3tDQ4Ol $2.99 Kindle $10.95 softcover

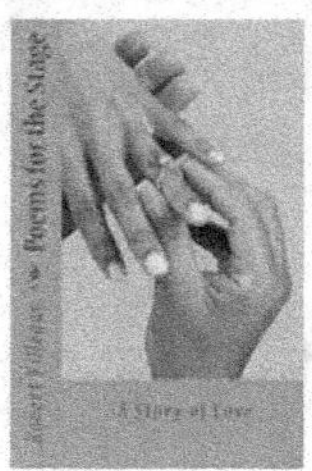 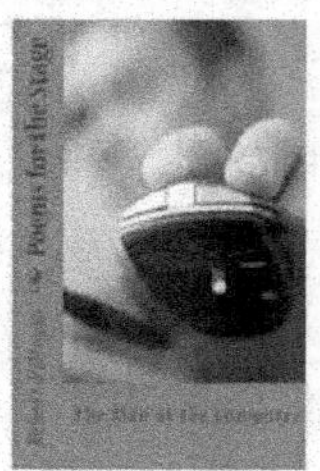

Poems for the Stage – A Story of Love

This dramatic presentation features poems found in Mr. Villegas's book Poetic Prose and Poetry. Some are also found in his book.

https://amzn.to/3gSJctV $2.99 Kindle $5.95 softcover

Poems for the Stage – The Man at the Computer

This dramatic presentation is based upon poems from Mr. Villegas's book Poetic Prose and Poetry. Some of the poems have been slightly altered to reflect the internal story. Mr. Villegas's book Poetic Prose and Poetry can be found on Amazon.com.

https://amzn.to/2R8zpFf $2.99 Kindle $5.95 softcover

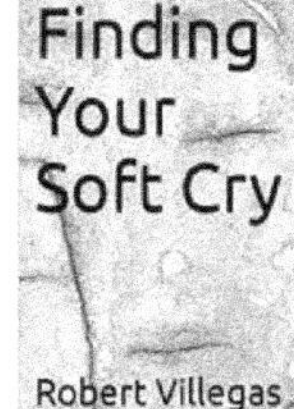

Naming Names in the NT

"Discovery consists of seeing what everybody has seen and thinking what nobody has thought." - Albert Szent-Gyogyi – 1937 Nobel Laureate https://amzn.to/3mXR66H $3.99 Kindle $9.95 softcover $16.95 hardcover

Finding Your Soft Cry

Every individual has a yearning to know that he is both free and good. This yearning comes to him from early youth, and he hopes that he eventually develops the intellectual tools to help him distinguish between his nature and the demands of society. The key to freedom is the ability to act without restriction and, especially, without guilt. https://amzn.to/3p8lY7m $3.99 Kindle $8.95 softcover $15.95 hardcover

The New Totalitarianism – Quo Vadis?

The previous century was one of the bloodiest in history. Two World Wars and many other wars do not bode well for our century that is beginning to rival the previous in its bloodlust. If we look carefully, we find in the last century the philosophical roots of the present century. The philosophers of the last century are the philosophers of the present. https://amzn.to/3AMZNFC $5.99 Kinde $10.95 softcover $25.95 hard cover

A Call to Reason

Is it possible that the problems in the world are not caused by capitalism and rich people? Is it possible that anti-capitalism and anti-reason philosophies are nothing more than elaborate hoaxes designed to convince people to give up everything they have honestly earned and take it away from them? Is it possible they are caused by the re-distribution of capital to wasteful uses and the consequent destruction of jobs and affluence? https://amzn.to/3mVNrq5 $5.99 Kindle $9.95 softcover $24.95 Hardcover